VIBRATIONAL
WEIGHT
RELEASE

KIDEST OM

Vibrational Weight Release by Kidest OM
3rd Edition

ISBN-13: 978-1495497759
ISBN-10: 1495497755

SELF RESPONSIBLITY

The author of this material does not dispense medical advice or prescribe the use of any technique as a form of professional therapeutic treatment for physical, emotional, psychological, or medical conditions without the advice of an appropriate qualified health practitioner or physician, either directly or indirectly. The intent of the author is only to offer information of a general nature. In the event you use any of the information in this material for yourself, which is your right, the author assumes no responsibility for your choices or actions. By using the material, you assume and accept full responsibility for any and all outcomes you experience.

*You cannot create lasting change
without expanding out of the
consciousness that brought forth the
things you want changed.*
- Kidest OM

CONTENTS

VIBRATIONAL WEIGHT RELEASE

The secret to lasting change is consciousness. A change in consciousness, a shift in the very mindset you hold and use to make sense of yourself and world is what translates into a changed experience, a new experience, a different reality. Experiencing a new body, a different reality around your physical body, requires you have a changed consciousness.

This book will take you through paradigm shifting information and a set of exercises so that you can build the body you want from the inside out. The book offers you new ways of looking at your entire physical system with a living intention that your new way of looking at your body will translate into a new experience of your body on all levels – in thought, in emotion, in imagination and in direct observation.

Each day you are provided with thoughts that allow you to look at your body from a new perspective. As you entertain these new ideas and practice the exercises offered over the course of 40 days, you will set into motion the shift in consciousness necessary to make any lasting change in this physical experience.

You *can* change your body from the inside out. You *can* create the body of your dreams.

Kidest OM

7

INTRODUCTION

Changing your body composition within the framework of deliberate creation is a different experience than changing your body within the existing mainstream "weight loss" paradigm. Deliberate creation requires that you take full ownership of the results you are getting. It requires that you take ownership of your energy, your mindset, your well-practiced patterns of thinking and feeling and work to change those areas within yourself first.

Deliberate creation says that you are getting what you are getting because you are being who you are being – meaning it is the well-rehearsed thoughts, feelings and points of observation that have gotten you what you're getting. The shift then is that your weight stops being about your behavior, habits and the external world, and it becomes about your consciousness – the preceding power out of which your habits, your behaviors and your observed experiences emerge.

The goal of this workbook is to offer you a framework of physical transformation that is based on creating a shift in consciousness first and allowing that shift to inform your new experiences of everything that relates to your body composition. In order to maximize what you gain from going through this workbook it's helpful to have a familiarity on the principles of reality creation.

To get the most out of this workbook and the environment of transformation it makes available, you must let go of having a body specific "result" in mind. You can absolutely set the intention that you will experience the shift in consciousness necessary to live the body of your dreams and let that pebble of intent drop into your heart, yet throughout the exercises and practices that follow, remain firmly fixed only on the goal of changing your consciousness around everything related to your body for your highest fulfilment. The main goal must be to have a significant shift in consciousness first and foremost.

The source and substance of your reality on every level is your interior, your internal world of thoughts, emotions, beliefs and so on. It is this interior space that is bringing about the experiences you are living in every facet of your life, and so it is the reorganization and transformation of this space that will allow you to experience something different.

Solely focus all of your energy in creating that shift in consciousness and let go of all other focus. Let nothing distract you from achieving that shift in consciousness, from changing your current energetic signature to one that ensures you bring about your desired experience of your body.

From this dedicated and continued focus on changing your consciousness, you are guaranteed to bring about the change necessary to live something different as it relates to your body. Go within and remain focused there intent only on building and integrating new patterns of thinking and feeling, while shedding old patterns of thinking and feeling. From that process of rebirthing in yourself a new mindset, a new consciousness, a new more coherent and resonant vibration, you will find yourself stepping into a new body and a new reality.

PART I: PREMISE OF WORKBOOK

∞ *Your body is a creation of your Consciousness.*

∞ *Your body is a recording or encoding of all the thoughts and feelings you have had about it in this lifetime.*

∞ *Your body's appearance and feel is a result of the beliefs, thoughts, and attitudes you have practiced about it.*

∞ *Your body is your practiced patterns of unique vibrations crystallized.*

∞ *Your body is the essence of your vibrational output congealed.*

∞ *Your body is an outcome of your dominant thought-force.*

∞ *Your body is constantly changing and morphing in accord to the blueprint set by your thoughts.*

∞ *You can shift the feel and pattern of your body naturally.*

• • •

These assertions emphasize the necessity of fully owning why you have the experience of your body that you currently do. They invite you to take full responsibility for the reality of the body that you are living. For as long as you attribute causation to circumstances and conditions outside of your own consciousness you give your power, and so ability to create and transform, away to factors you make up in your mind as being out of your control.

The primacy of your own consciousness must be established in all that you are living.

IT'S ALL CONSCIOUSNESS

Consciousness is what permeates every dimension of your entire reality matrix. What empowers the creative energies of your reality is you.

You are consciousness observing, integrating, and bringing into visibility realities that are in harmony about what you have decided is true and valid.

You are who endows thoughts with truth power.

You are what energizes and empowers thought forces with your attention.

You are who gives meaning, significance, and value to every thought that arises in awareness.

You and what you give attention and validity to is at the root of all that materializes as your physical body and world in each and every moment.

Within your powerful awareness of Being, within your experience of existing, are an endless array of thoughts, beliefs, attitudes.

These thoughts and beliefs, these silent stories that are continuously active and floating around in your awareness are energetic patterns with their own unique quality, tone, and resonance. And it is these energetic patterns that determine the look and feel about everything in your physical world, including your immediate seemingly ever-present physical body.

Put another way, energy in constant motion, particles vibrating and resonating at various frequencies, particles that are popping in and out of existence are what construct and bring into visibility the world and physical body that you experience moment after moment. So your reality and experience of your physical body is really a result of the balance of these vibrational creative powers that you keep activated and energized within yourself through your belief in their realness, truth value, and validity.

It is you who gives your current experience continuity by validating it and projecting it ahead of you or in front of you. It is you who values your current landscape so much that you invest into it all of your energy. It is you who gives it a sense of permanence and un-changeability. It is you who does all this and more, and so it is you who can take all that attribution of validity, realness and continuity away.

As your physical body is made up of

energy, since your physical body is itself a field of frequencies vibrating in a specific way, it stands to reason that it too is in a constant state of motion. Every particle that creates the appearance of your physical body is right now in this moment fluctuating at great speed and it is only because your physical senses are not calibrated to show you this experience, that your body appears solid, fixed, and static to you.

Pay attention to how it is that you come to be aware of your body. You, as awareness, register a series of sensations and refer to those sensations in some way to tell you that you have a body. When you deprive the senses of any input there is no awareness of the body, there is just awareness. You experience this every day when you sleep.

You also know your body through learned and inherited concepts. What are your fingers when you stop calling them and knowing them as "fingers"? The arbitrary partitioning of the physical body into conceptual parts and the definitions imposed upon the unified system create artificial standards for how the body operates. When you treat the body and observe the body as parts (legs, arms, stomach, hair etc.) you prevent yourself from noticing that it actually has no such boundaries – it is a unified system.

When you perceive the body as being fixed, solid and unchanging, bringing about any level of transformation will take work. When you perceive the body as being a field of energy and information that is constantly and continuously being altered, as a sequence of images, sensations and sounds appearing within you, then transcending (ending the trance) of any pattern becomes immediate and definite. A shift in consciousness is not hard work. With the right information, focus, and intent on your part, you can bring your desired shifts readily and effortlessly.

With this understanding, with this dawning realization, you can see the power of engaging in vibrational weight release. Consciousness is what materializes. Consciousness is what matters. And so it is a significant and meaningful shift in consciousness that will allow you to experience your desired outcome.

Allowing This Text to Work

Every thought-form you empower manifests itself as the circumstances and conditions of your physical life. Your body is no exception to this universal creative process. This text is designed to help you access and form new patterns of thought around your body, so you can begin to materialize and experience your desired physical body.

Your practiced vibration which shows itself as your thoughts, beliefs, and attitudes, has everything to do with why your body feels and appears as it does, for above all else, the very atoms that construct your physical body respond first and foremost to the consciousness that you are. It's imperative that you accept the premise "my body is a reflection of my vibration".

In this lifetime, you have created many thought patterns, beliefs, and attitudes, around food, exercise, your appearance, your figure, and around many other aspects of your physical body which you constantly play on loop in your mind – which you constantly activate and empower in the field of consciousness that you are. <u>You have an ongoing silent story you tell about your body in the privacy of your own mind. You have an ongoing vibrational output when it comes to your physical body.</u>

You are in the constant company of thoughts.

Every time you sit to eat food, you are thinking thoughts and so resonating in a particular way. Every time you walk down the grocery aisle, you are thinking thoughts. Every time you walk up a flight of stairs, you are thinking thoughts. Every time you take a walk anywhere or anytime you decide not to engage in any kind of physical activity, you are thinking thoughts. Every time you walk by a mirror, you are thinking thoughts.

Everything you do, you do so in the constant and endless company of your thoughts. You are constantly and continuously resonating, vibrating, and radiating waves of energy. If weight-release is your goal, if shifting your physical appearance is your goal, then it's important that your thoughts or your overall vibration supports, empowers, and mobilizes that goal into materialization in an irreversible way rather than contradict it. For in this vibration-based reality matrix, the thoughts you constantly think and the feelings you tune into and anchor have more power to bring you the results you want in a permanent and effortless way than any action based effort you involve yourself in.

Your goals do not need to feel like a struggle. Your process of achievement on every subject need not feel like a struggle. In fact, the only reason that it does feel like a struggle is because you have contradictory thoughts playing in your mind every step of the way. You have vibrational resistance built up, and that kind of resistance is the only reason why your results are slow to come and difficult to maintain. So what if you could be in perfect harmony with what you desire to experience as your physical body? What if you could completely harmonize with your desired physical body right now in this moment?

Working with your thought patterns, creating shifts at the vibrational level of your being, is essentially treating the root cause of your physical world rather than trying to adjust the manifested outcome. Beating your desires into manifestation does not give you lasting results. Struggling to bring about shifts does not support the premise that you are a powerful unlimited being with the resources of endless dimensions available to you.

This text contains a series of exercises for you to engage in daily over the next 40 days. As you go through the text you will expose your negative practiced patterns of thought to yourself, and as you practice and create new patterns of thinking, you will shift and expand out of the consciousness that created what you want to change. You will find your goals easily met.

Engage yourself in this text daily. Commit to change your inner template. Do all the exercises and allow yourself to dwell on and practice the new thoughts you are offered. For as you do, you will begin to think in a completely new way about your physical body and will experience the immediate and long-term effects of that shift in your consciousness. You will begin to feel good about your body in many ways, and feeling good about your body is always the prime indicator that you are on the path to true and lasting fulfillment.

You may wonder why 40 days. It is through repeated contact that a stranger becomes your friend. It is through repeated contact with new ideas that they become familiar and second-nature to you. When you consistently give a new idea your attention, you flow energy into that idea until it is dense enough for it to "solidify" and integrate into your conscious outlook.

Repetition is and has been the pattern of everything you've learned. Everything you right now know is an idea you've repeatedly entertained and accepted – from tying your shoes to your views about this world, everything is an idea you have practiced and habituated. So the integration process requires your unbroken attention for a given period of time. Both in the traditions of the East and the West, 40 days is held to be the length of time to set in motion such a transformation. And so that rule-set is being applied to this text also. It's important that you go through this text with perfect continuity at least the first time through.

Your Body: An Upgrade in Paradigm

How do you see, smell, touch, hear, taste?
How do you come to sense anything?
How do you come to perceive everything
around you?
What is the cause of your body?

The Electrical Circuit-Board

On the physical level, your body is made
up of electrically charged nerve wires and
trillions of cells that are in constant and
continuous communication, through the
exchange of energy currents. Energy currents
carrying information and feedback are
continuously transmitted within your physical
body.

You perceive your external environment,
including your body, through the information
conveyed in this electrical or vibrational
information exchange. Your very perception of
your body, how you perceive and receive your
body through your physical senses, is taken in
through the exchange of this electrical or
vibrational information. So everything you

experience as your body is a vibrational interpretation – a reading of electrical signals.

Your brain is constantly interpreting and assimilating this electrical information so that you form and perceive your body as the solid material of flesh and bones you take it to be. Yet everything about you is a translation of this vibrational or electrical information. What you see as your body is a vibrational experience. What you feel as your body, what you touch, any information you have about your body is a vibrational translation of electrical data.

The Intelligent System

Nothing about your physical body requires or has ever required your conscious input. The intelligence of your body is so vast that a single cell has transformed and morphed itself into the gathering of trillions of cells your developed adult body now stands at.

There are more automatic processes (from breathing to digesting to regenerating) going on in your body right now than you can consciously fathom. There are endless and automatic chemical processes going on in your body right in this very instant without your conscious direction or input. Every cell and every nerve wire, every packet of energy that forms your body, knows exactly its function and place in the physical system. No exceptions. Your body is designed to be and operates as a self-created and self-generating intelligent mechanism.

A System of Constant Change

Your physical body is made up of vibrating packets of energy that are in constant and continuous motion and communication. It is made up of energy-waves and information with an unfathomable intelligence and function.

There is nothing about your body that is as still, static, and solid as it appears to your senses. The appearance of a solid body is only an illusion of the senses. And so treating and thinking of your body in those terms in no way serves your ability to experience its intelligence and miraculous nature.

What you perceive as your feet, what you perceive as your shoulder, what you perceive as your hands, all of it is actually a movement of energy. Everything about your body is right now in rapid vibration. Your entire body is energy in constant and ceaseless motion. Under the right magnification, all that appears as your body is an arrangement of wave patterns and empty space. And it is from this angle of perception that you want to engage to bring about your desired shifts.

A Responsive System

Everything in your body is responsive first and foremost to your thoughts, to your vibrational commands. Every thought you think, every thought-force you breathe life into through your attachment or investment in it, is a message you give to the energy packets that make up your physical system. Every thought is a command your body obeys. Every thought carries an electrical charge, every thought carries information the particles of your body decode and encode onto themselves.

Your body is constantly and continuously recording the messages in your thoughts, listening and obeying the unconscious commands you are constantly directing to it. By current estimates, you think approximately 70,000 thoughts in a given day. You give that many commands in a given day. Think about this. Take a look at your body through a new lens. Take a moment to consider the information in this text and see your body in a new light.

Questions to Ask Yourself

What about my body is fixed?

What about my body is static?

What about my body is unchanging?

What about my body is not in constant motion?

What about my body is not in rapid movement?

Am I aware that my body is energy in constant motion?

Exposing Your Rule-Sets

∞ *What are your criteria for weight release?*

∞ *What do you believe it takes to release weight permanently?*

∞ *How many days, months does it take?*

∞ *How much work does it take?*

∞ *How many calories do you need to consume or burn?*

∞ *How rapidly can you permanently release weight?*

∞ *How long do you believe it takes to drop the pounds from your reality?*

∞ *Will you keep your new weight after you release those pounds?*

∞ *What will that take?*

Ask yourself these questions and more questions like them. Get a deeper look at the rule-sets you've created for yourself – the thought parameters you've practiced about weight release and what it takes.

You will always create and materialize your experiences within the boundaries of your beliefs so it's crucial that you expose and make visible to yourself these beliefs. These rule-sets are not facts. They are not solid unchangeable realities. In a vibrational reality, in a world of energy in constant motion, the only rules there are, are the one's you've constructed through your dominant beliefs. All your current criteria for weight release are only thoughts that have been practiced. They are only thoughts that have been used to materialize energy into form. They are only thought-forms, specific patterns of energy that have been used to shape your experience of reality. And they are only as valid and powerful as you make them.

Your body will always respond first to your practiced patterns of thought – to the invisible expectations and conditions you've formed and set based on information you've gathered and integrated into your own unique outlook in your physical experience. The more you make these beliefs or manufactured expectations visible to yourself, the more you can deliberately change them so that getting the results you want is effortless and natural.

Food & You

What is food?

What is food made of?

How does your body process food?

What determines your body's ability to process food?

Let's face it, with food being a part of your daily experience, you have accumulated a great many thoughts about it. Food is one of the areas connected to the body in which many people have built a great deal of resistance around. You have split your food into "good for me" and "bad for me" categories so most of the time when you're sitting down to eat, the many thoughts you have on loop in your mind are tormenting you about what you're about to put into your body. If feelings of guilt, shame, disappointment and the like arise within you around your relationship with food, these are indicators of faulty beliefs around yourself, your body and your world being in operation.

If your relationship to food falls on the spectrum between addiction and avoidance, where you are either relying on food to meet needs other than nutrition and fuel or you are avoiding food to the point you are denying your body nutrition and fuel, this again is an indication of faulty beliefs around yourself, your body and your world being in operation. Left to its own wisdom, without the interference of your learned or inherited beliefs, your body innately knows exactly what it needs and when it needs it. Your body knows exactly the composition it needs to be at its best in its natural environment – its natural environment being one that is free of your emotionally driven addictive and avoidance behaviors.

Every thought you accept internally as true, real or valid is a command, so while you sit to eat, you are giving your body messages that are often contradictory to your desired goal. Food and eating then and what you begin to cycle within yourself when you are around food or about to eat, is an area worthy of your conscious engagement for the simple reason that this is a big part of your physical well-being. If you hoard food, if you buy multiple packages of the same thing, if you need to have stashes of it in nearby drawers, if you restrict yourself and obsessively count calories and macros, you want to take a look at the thoughts, beliefs, and emotions behind all of these behaviors. The behaviors in and of themselves are neither desirable nor undesirable – what you want to look at is the energy behind them. If you are operating out of and behaving from empowerment, intention, love and appreciation for yourself and your body, and other positive energies your results and experiences will mirror that energy. If you are operating from fear, disempowerment, scarcity, lack, shame, guilt, frustration and the like, then the energies at work will yield more things for you to feel fear, disempowerment, scarcity, lack, shame, guilt, frustration and the like about yourself, your body and your world.

As you begin this journey then, question your habits and behaviors. Take a look and see why it is that you do what you do, why it is that you think what you think, why it is that you feel what you feel around food and eating. Look behind the curtain of your own habits and face the operating patterns of thinking and feeling.

There is an abundance of food varieties in your experience. There are so many food groups, recipes, colors, names, for you to choose from. And all of these food varieties are also patterns of energy, patterns of light and information, unique vibrational offerings you bring to yourself and your body. The food you consume like everything else in your reality is a vibrational offering you bring to yourself and your body.

And so you want to expand your awareness around your relationship with food. You want to bring your awake awareness to your relationship to food and eating. You want to ask yourself questions to really know where you are vibrating in regards to food and eating.

∞ Are you in harmony with the food you consume?

∞ Are you in complete resonance with the food you consume?

∞ Are you inspired, excited, and delighted about what you're about to eat when you sit down to eat?

∞ Or is food yet another unconscious process for you?

The energy you bring to the table with you, the energy you bring when you're picking out or preparing your food, where you are resonating and vibrating with all the food you come into contact with absolutely affects how your body then processes and responds to the food. Begin to bring an awareness to your dining table, your kitchen, your grocery stores, your markets, your office cafeteria, your restaurants and anywhere else where food and eating occur. Begin to see just exactly what stories you're activating and empowering within yourself. See if you are energized internally when you think about food and all that is related to it in your experience. See the level of elevation or depression of energy that arises when you are around food, thinking about food, and engaging in activities around eating.

Think about the kinds of messages you're constantly giving to your body around food. Make a conscious effort to change your thinking around food. Make a conscious commitment to be aware of your charged thoughts around food. Take a moment, just two or three minutes, before at least one of your meals during the course of your day to deliberately come into resonance with, to harmonize with good-feeling thoughts, which are thoughts vibrating at a higher frequency, on the subject of food and your body.

Do this consistently over the next 40 days to habituate this kind of thinking and promote a deeper awareness that supports a much more harmonious relationship to the food you offer your body and your being. Do this deliberate energetic shift before at least one of your meals every day.

Think and resonate with thoughts like:

∞   I am so grateful for this food offering before me.

∞   I love and appreciate the energy this food

will provide for my body.

∞ My body will so appreciate what I'm about to eat.

∞ I love how my body thrives on all foods.

∞ Every day and in every way I grow more and more attracted to the food that nourishes and fuels my body.

∞ What an amazing creative expression is this plate of food!

∞ How wonderful is it to have such a delicious meal before me!

∞ It's amazing that my body knows exactly how to extract what it needs from what I'm about to eat. I love my body's intelligence.

∞ I love how my body will know what to do with whatever food I put on my plate.

∞ I so appreciate how my body understands more about the content of these foods than I do.

∞ It is so amazing that my body already knows what minerals and nutrients it's going to process from this food.

∞ I love how my body will convert this food into the energy it needs to maintain its balance and well-being.

∞ My body is so intelligent.

∞ I love, love, love my body's intelligence.

∞ I'm so appreciative of all that my body does for me.

∞ I love nourishing my body.

∞ My body is so extraordinary at all the functions it carries out so automatically, easily, and effortlessly.

∞ I love my body. It is such an intelligent flawless expression of infinite wellness.

∞ I intend to let my body do what it innately knows to do.

∞ I intend to support my body's intelligence by thinking good feeling supportive thoughts like these.

∞ I love being in harmony with my food.

∞ I love being in harmony with my body's innate knowing.

∞ I love how my body guides me to exactly what it needs.

∞ I love knowing that food is energy.

∞ I so appreciate that the cells of my body are cooperative and compliant to my desired body image.

∞ I am always relaxed about food now. I know that the way my body responds to the food I eat is determined by the thoughts I have practiced.

∞ It is so amazing that my body formed itself out of a single cell, into these trillions of cells without any input from me or anyone else.

∞ I'm going to trust the intelligence of my body.

∞ I'm going to support that intelligence by choosing these good feeling thoughts.

∞ All is well relative to me and food.

∞ I love knowing that how I feel about food is only thoughts I have practiced.

∞ I so appreciate realizing that my beliefs about food are only thoughts I have practiced.

It's really the little thoughts you have practiced along the way that form themselves into the resistant patterns or negative beliefs that flare up anytime you're about to eat. It's the day to day thoughts that you've thought, and that is something you can change intentionally and consciously.

If resistance arises as you go through this workbook or you experience thoughts of all that you have to give up or all that you're going to have to start doing, recognize that this is stepping out of the goal of this workbook.

The goal here is not about having you giving up old behaviors and starting up new ones. The goal here is to only change the thinking and feeling patterns that have been at work up until now. That's it. You don't have to change any external behaviors. You don't have to force yourself to stop or start anything. Right here and right now, this is just about doing some cleaning up, updating, and rearranging of your internal stuff. Once you do the vibrational cleanup and update, once you change your energy, whatever behaviors that need to be different will shift on their own. There is no force here. There is only flow.

PART II – THE WORKBOOK

Each day contains a thought for you to contemplate followed by exercises for you to take part in as you go on about your day. There is a MORNING PROCESS and an EVENING PROCESS that you take yourself through over the course of 40 days. If the ideas offered in this text are new for you, you can take yourself through the text multiple times and repeat the process until you feel the shift in consciousness – which you will literally feel and notice.

Ideally you'll do the MORNING PROCESS first thing in the morning so that you begin to tune into and steer yourself toward this new way of thinking when your mind or brain waves are still in receptive mode.

For the same reason, it's ideal to do the EVENING PROCESS before you go to sleep. Processing information when your brain/mind is least active and preoccupied means you'll be able to give this material the kind of attention that's necessary to make a shift in your consciousness.

Things you'll need:

1) This text.
2) Your commitment to change.

3) A journal to process this information, practice the new thoughts, and keep a record of your insights.

Questions to Ask Yourself Frequently

What about my body is fixed?

What about my body is static?

What about my body is unchanging?

What about my body is not in constant motion?

What about my body is not in rapid movement?

Am I aware that my body is energy in constant motion?

Daily Exercises

Thought of the Day: Every stream of thought you tune into is vibrating at a unique frequency and so offers you a unique resonance to attune to. Each day of the following text contains a train of thought for you to contemplate and consider so that you can begin resonating at a different frequency altogether when it comes to your body.

The best way to shift your consciousness on a given subject is to shift your belief system around that subject – build a new understanding of what your body is and what it does. These daily thoughts are aimed at doing just that by offering you a new way of vibrating, a new way of resonating in looking and thinking about your physical body.

When you transform your mind, when you transform or shift your dominant vibration, you absolutely transform everything in your world.

New Thoughts to Practice: Each day you're also given new thoughts to practice – a list of affirmation-like thoughts you can engage in. Let yourself cycle these thoughts.

Combined with the daily thought you contemplate, the new thoughts you practice will allow you to form and radiate a new understanding, a new vibrational pattern. Write these new thoughts out several times and let yourself remember them as you go on about your day. Feel and experience them with your whole body. Let every cell in your body, let every atom of your body, plug into the energy of these thoughts. If other new thoughts about your body come to you, add them to your daily list.

Paying Attention – throughout each day it's important to pay attention to the thoughts you are thinking around your physical body. Wherever you are, set the intention to be aware of what you're thinking.

Your emotions will always indicate to you the quality or essence of your thoughts so use your emotions to tell you what your balance of thinking is. If you are feeling negative emotion, if you are feeling uncomfortable, at any point during the day, this negative emotion is indicating to you that you are thinking thoughts in opposition to what you are wanting. Make note of that. Make note of what you're cycling within yourself when it comes to your body, food, movement, and anything else that has to do with how your body looks and feels.

Pre-Meal Shifting – As food is a big part of your focus when it comes to your physical body, it's important to be conscious of your thoughts around food.

Each day contains a reminder to re-train your thinking and shift your vibration around food and how you approach it. If you can shift your energy around food, if you can stretch and relax your mental muscles around the food you are about to eat before you eat by thinking good feeling thoughts, you will transform your relationship with food and in turn transform how your physical body responds to the food you eat. It's always in the thoughts you've been practicing every step of the way.

Visualize/Day Dream: Visualizing is a great way to radiate the kind of energy that is in line with what you want. You cannot get to a good feeling body when your constant focus is a body you have accumulated many negative feelings around. So visualization is a great way to take yourself into the energy of your desired body.

What will it feel like when you reach your goal? What kind of clothes will you wear? What do you look like? Spend five minutes or so visualizing your new look. Feel the feelings. Picture yourself wearing something you've been wanting to wear. What will people say to you when they see you? What will you say to yourself when you look in the mirror? Step into the energy by tuning into the picture of your desired outcome.

Positive Focus: often times, through habit, you may focus on what you perceive to be "wrong" with your body. By default the mind wonders and focuses on everything you don't like about your body.

Take this moment to think about everything that is right with your body right now just as it is. Deliberately bring yourself to focus on what you like about it, what you love about it. Focus on your body's intelligence. Focus on your body's effortless way of being, how it does all that it does so powerfully well. Come into a sense of appreciating and loving everything about your body. Deliberately train yourself into positive focus. Not only will this shift your dominant thought patterns but it will also shift the energy or essence you radiate outward.

Appreciating: The energy of appreciation is one of the highest frequencies you can access and attune yourself to deliberately. The higher the energies you attune to, the more effortlessly and fluidly the things you are wanting flow into your experience. Appreciation of anything really gives you the power to instantly shift dimensions.

The cells of your body, the particles that form your body, are carrying on an infinite number of processes without your conscious direction or participation. You breathe without thinking about it. Your heart beats without your having to do anything about it. Your body digests and processes the food you eat without your thinking about it. Your body distributes all the oxygen and minerals needed through all the systems in your body without your conscious effort. Your eyes are working for you. Your ears are working for you. Your legs, your arms, every aspect of your body is working for you effortlessly and constantly without your having to think about it and direct it.

Take a moment, 2 or 3 minutes each day, to appreciate everything your body does for you. No matter how it looks or feels, it is still automatically and effortlessly carrying on an infinite number of processes that you don't have to do anything about. Take this time to take your awareness through your body and appreciate it for how it serves you day in and day out. Let the last note at the end of your day be your appreciation for your whole physical system.

Questions to Ask Yourself Frequently

What about my body is fixed?

What about my body is static?

What about my body is unchanging?

What about my body is not in constant motion?

What about my body is not in rapid movement?

Am I aware that my body is energy in constant motion?

SUGGESTED GUIDELINES

1) As a rule, it's important to keep your deliberate effort to shift your consciousness on your chosen subject to yourself. Keep it as your secret so as not to introduce the negative/limiting/resistant patterns of thought active in other's into your efforts. This is your work and yours alone so mind the kind of input you allow into your efforts. Be mindful of who and in what way you share your commitment to make the internal shift with.

2) These efforts aren't about making anything happen. You no more have to make what you're wanting happen than you have to pull the grass out of the ground or manually rotate the earth on its axis. There are natural laws at work here and you are merely working with those laws by releasing your practiced patterns of resistance. You really don't need to hammer anything into place so let your focus only be on changing your patterns of thought, shifting your vibration. The natural outcome of fulfillment is inevitable.

3) Keep conscious note that appreciation of all the things you already have on every subject is the quickest way to open your energy channels and increase the flow. Resistance in the way of critical thoughts, doubtful thoughts, and the like only serve to block or pinch off the flow of universal energy. Appreciate! Appreciate! Appreciate!

4) Keep your attention on the Cause of everything you experience. Do not be swayed by the outcomes, the conditions manifested around you. All conditions and circumstances are rapidly changing things, they are already dissolving the instant you decide to flow your energy elsewhere. The Cause is always your consciousness, and the thoughts you have encoded yourself with. Resolve to work at the level of Cause.

5) Relieve yourself from determining or deciding how your desires will manifest. The HOW is none of your business. Allow the Universe, from its broader all-seeing vantage point, to flow it to you through easy and accessible channels. It's not your work to figure out "how" anything will come to you or materialize into your view. Your only job is to ask through the thoughts you radiate and then get out of the way.

6) Remind yourself that fulfillment is your birthright just because you exist. There is absolutely nothing that you cannot become or materialize. "Impossible" is not a word or concept known by the energy that builds this Universe. Line yourself up to that omni-possibility. If life, if this Universe has inspired you to conceive of a desire, that desire can absolutely materialize. There are no exceptions.

7) Take time out of the equation. The only place is here and the only time is now. Whatever your desire, it can only materialize in the Now. There is no future moment. There is no future time of tomorrow, later, or "in six months" for your desire to be visible to you. The only place and time for it to materialize, is right here and right now. Be mindful of the mental tendency to futurize and set up a condition of time for materialization. Now is all there is.

8) Think of this 40 day process as a way to "upgrade" your mental operating system. It's really not anything more mystical or abstract. You're simply re-writing the thoughts you've embedded or programmed your mind with up until now.

9) Be consistent and be patient with yourself and your practice. It takes a buildup of energy in consciousness to materialize into the physical so let your intention be to make that necessary shift in consciousness. Allow yourself to take in information along the lines of creating change from the inside out. There are endless resources and information available that you can make use of to fill your mind with the type of thoughts necessary to make such a shift.

10) Bring yourself to keep focusing on what it is that you do want. Decide to supply and apply your power, your energy only to what it is you're wanting to see. Commit to yourself and your vision. Say to yourself each day "today, no matter where I go or what I do, I choose to flow my energy only to those things I am wanting. I choose my vision." You are always radiating the energy of the thing that has your attention the most, so let what captivates you be the thing that you want.

Day 1

Thought of the day: the trillions of intelligent cells that make up your body, which themselves are made up of particles that are in constant motion, are continuously morphing into the body that you see. The structure they follow into how to form your body is the beliefs you have been practicing in this lifetime. As you change these beliefs, you change the blueprint your cells use to build your body in every moment. Your body is an in-the-moment creation of your consciousness.

Pre-meal Shifting: make an effort to do the Pre-meal Shifting exercise at least at one of your meals today.

MORNING PROCESS

1. Contemplate the thought of the day.

2. **Practice New Thoughts:** let yourself cycle these thoughts. Write them out several times and let yourself repeat them as you go on about your day. If new thoughts about your body come to you, add them to your daily list.

- The cells of my body always respond to the positive thoughts I think.
- My body serves me well.
- My body responds to my intention and to my attention.
- My body thrives on all foods.
- My body is very resilient.

3. **Visualize/Day Dream:** What will it feel like when you reach your goal? What kind of clothes will you wear? Spend five minutes or so visualizing your new look. Feel the feelings. Picture yourself wearing something you've been wanting to wear. What will people say to you when they see you? What will you say to yourself when you look in the mirror?

EVENING PROCESS

1. Contemplate the thought of the day and record your feelings, insights, and reactions.

2. Practice New Thoughts

3. **Positive Focus:** Write 10 new things you like about your body right now in your

journal.

4. Appreciate! Appreciate! Appreciate!

Day 2

Thought of the day: your body is made up of trillions of cells that are cooperating with one another to form the body that you see, feel, and sense right now. These conscious intelligent cells are also cooperating with you and the balance of your thoughts. Your communication with these cells is always taking place through your dominant habits of thought – through the thoughts you repeat and practice.

Every thought you think is a thought you practice. As you tip the balance of your thoughts toward the support of your desired weight, every single cell, every single particle that makes up your body will cooperate with your new belief structure without fail. Your physical body is the cooperative outcome of your thoughts and these trillions of intelligent cells.

Pre-meal Shifting: make an effort to do the Pre-meal Shifting exercise at least at one of your meals today.

MORNING PROCESS

1. Contemplate the thought of the day

2. Practice New Thoughts:

- The better my thoughts about my body feel, the closer I am to materializing my goal.
- There is an absolute correlation between the thoughts I think about my body, how I feel about my body, and how I experience my body.
- I am now consciously choosing the kinds of thoughts I think and so I am deliberately affecting the feel and look of my body.
- My physical appearance is simply an outcome of my chronic thoughts.
- I can always choose better feeling thoughts about my body, about anything.

3. **Visualize/Day Dream:** What will it feel like when you reach your goal? What kind of clothes will you wear? Spend five minutes or so visualizing your new look. Feel the feelings. Picture yourself wearing something you've been wanting to wear. What will people say to you when they see you? What will you say to yourself when you look in

the mirror?

EVENING PROCESS

1. Contemplate the thought of the day and
    record your feelings, insights, and reactions.

2. Practice New Thoughts

3. **Positive Focus:** Write 10 new things you
    like about your body right now in your
    journal.

4. **Appreciate! Appreciate! Appreciate!**

Day 3

Thought of the day: Everything always comes down to the thoughts you think. Thought is the basic building block of every aspect of your physical experience. That includes metabolism! What do you think determines whether you have a high or low metabolism? What is metabolism? It is the thoughts you think that always determine how energy moves through your body and how energy materializes as your body.

Every thought you think vibrates at a particular frequency. And your body already has a built-in indicator of what that frequency is. Good feelings are telling you that you are in that moment thinking thoughts of "higher" frequencies. So the better your thoughts feel, the higher or faster the particles of your body are vibrating and the more life-energy is moving through you.

Metabolism is nothing more than the way energy is moving through your body and materializing as everything that makes up your body. And what slows it down or what speeds the energy movement is always your habit of thought. Shift out of the beliefs that say metabolism declines. Shift out of someone else's decision to observe their body's ability to metabolize energy as something that can decrease or slow down.

Pre-meal Shifting: make an effort to do the Pre-meal Shifting exercise at least at one of your meals today.

MORNING PROCESS

1. Contemplate the thought of the day and record your feelings, insights, and reactions.

2. Practice New Thoughts:

   - I have the power to change my thought patterns.
   - My physical body is an amazingly intelligent living system.
   - There are so many important functions that my body carries out without my

conscious involvement.

- My body knows how to do so much all on its own.
- My metabolism is the best it has ever been.

3. **Visualize/Day Dream:** What will it feel like when you reach your goal? What kind of clothes will you wear? Spend five minutes or so visualizing your new look. Feel the feelings. Picture yourself wearing something you've been wanting to wear. What will people say to you when they see you? What will you say to yourself when you look in the mirror?

EVENING PROCESS

1. Contemplate the thought of the day and record your feelings, insights, and reactions.

2. Practice New Thoughts

3. **Positive Focus:** Write 10 things you like about your body right now.

4. **Appreciate! Appreciate! Appreciate!**

Day 4

Thought of the day: it's important that you shift your focus more toward the body you are wanting to see rather than the body you see right now. As often as you can let yourself live in the feeling of already having your desired body in every way. The more you dwell on what you don't like about your body, what you think it lacks, what you don't want, or how unhappy you are about it, the more you draw to yourself more of what you don't want and further crystallize the chronic thought and emotional patterns that aren't supporting your goal.

Everything you think pulses through your body and radiates outward from you – you are constantly broadcasting the energy or essence of your thoughts from your being, and the Universe is responding that same essence back to you.

You are also constantly sending signals to your body through your patterns of emotionalized thinking – you are in constant communication with your body. You are in constant communication with the environment, the Universe. So train yourself into emitting the essence of what you do want to experience. Train yourself into radiating appreciation, happiness, joy, love, and other good feeling energies so that the Universe responds by giving you experiences that will continue to evoke those energies from you, and your body responds by reshaping itself to reflect your vision.

Let yourself dwell on what you will look like. Let yourself imagine and pretend and feel the reality of your desired level of fitness, health, size and shape. As you do this, you will literally shift your dominant thought patterns and re-wire your brain, creating new neuronal networks that are in support of what you are wanting to experience.

Every thought you think, every image you dwell on, is doing much more for you than you realize.

Pre-meal Shifting: make an effort to do the Pre-meal Shifting exercise at least at one of your meals today.

MORNING PROCESS

1. Contemplate the thought of the day.

2. Practice New Thoughts:

- I trust the intelligence of my body and I support it with my positive thoughts.
- My body serves me so well.
- My body is always moving toward wellness.
- My body is extraordinary and miraculous in the way it functions.
- I have the ability to find and maintain good feeling thoughts around my body.

3. Visualize/Day Dream

EVENING PROCESS

1. Contemplate the thought of the day and record your feelings, insights, and reactions.

2. Practice New Thoughts

3. **Positive Focus:** Write 10 things you like about your body right now.

4. **Appreciate!** Appreciate! Appreciate!

Day 5

Thought of the day: left to its own intelligence, your body can thrive and amaze you to no end. Your body is neither vulnerable nor fragile. Just dwell on what your body is made of right now. There are literally trillions of cells communicating and cooperating with one another in a way that really don't require or involve any input from you.

Your chronic negative thought habits introduce static in your body's ability to communicate, summon and process the energy that it needs. It is only your chronic negative thought patterns that interfere with the intelligent and effortless functioning of your physical body.

So with every new good-feeling thought you think and practice you are letting your body's natural ability to transform itself and its resilience come to the forefront.

Pre-meal Shifting: make an effort to do the Pre-meal Shifting exercise at least at one of your meals today.

MORNING PROCESS

1. Contemplate the thought of the day and record your feelings, insights, and reactions.

2. Practice New Thoughts:

   - I appreciate my body.
   - There are far more things going right with my body than I realize.
   - My body is a reflection of the thoughts I think.
   - My body is a reflection of my chronic thought patterns.
   - My body will always reflect the changes in my thinking.

3. **Visualize/Day Dream:** What will it feel like when you reach your goal? What kind of clothes will you wear? Spend five minutes or so visualizing your new look. Feel the feelings. Picture yourself wearing something you've been wanting to wear. What will people say to you when they see you? What will you say to yourself when you look in the mirror?

EVENING PROCESS

1. Contemplate the thought of the day and record your feelings, insights, and reactions.

2. **Practice New Thoughts**

3. **Positive Focus:** Write 10 things you like about your body right now.

4. **Appreciate!** Appreciate! Appreciate!

Day 6

Thought of the day: your body is actually a gathering or grouping of particles that are in constant motion right in this instant. Your body and every aspect of it is made of energy. Every one of the cells of your body are themselves composed of cooperative vibrating particles. Dwell on that. Take a moment to look at your body and recognize that every aspect of your physical body is right now made of rapidly moving particles. There is nothing that is static about your body. There is nothing that is unchanging about your body. There is nothing that is fixed about your body. Change, constant change, is a natural and constant part of your physical body.

And how easily you experience this rapid change is a result of the thoughts you have practiced, the belief walls you have created.

Pre-meal Shifting: make an effort to do the Pre-meal Shifting exercise at least at one of your meals today.

MORNING PROCESS

1. **Contemplate the thought of the day.**

2. **Practice New Thoughts:** let yourself cycle these thoughts. Write them out several times and let yourself repeat them as you go on about your day. If new thoughts about your body come to you, add them to your daily list.

    - I always have more power to affect my experience than I realize.
    - I feel wonderful thinking about my improved size and shape.
    - I love feeling good about my body and its intelligent nature.
    - My body is not a clump of flesh and bones, it is a gathering of conscious and constantly active cells.
    - The particles of my body are always in constant motion, nothing about my body is fixed, unchanging, and static.

3. **Visualize/Day Dream:** What will it feel like when you reach your goal? What kind of clothes will you wear? Spend five minutes or so visualizing your new look. Feel the

feelings. Picture yourself wearing something you've been wanting to wear. What will people say to you when they see you? What will you say to yourself when you look in the mirror?

EVENING PROCESS

1. Contemplate the thought of the day and record your feelings, insights, and reactions.

2. Practice New Thoughts

3. **Positive Focus:** Write 10 things you like about your body right now.

4. **Appreciate!** Appreciate! Appreciate!

Day 7

Thought of the day: your body is an extraordinary mechanism that is attentive and responsive to your thoughts. It will be whatever you request it to be for it is always cooperating with the asking of your thoughts. It will be whatever you allow it to be for it is always conforming to the request of your thoughts. It will be whatever you want it to be for it is always responding to the assertions of your thoughts. Your body will be whatever you EXPECT it to be, and your expectation of your body is formed through the thoughts you have practiced. As you practice new thoughts, you create new expectations for your physical body. And it will absolutely conform to that.

Pre-meal Shifting: make an effort to do the Pre-meal Shifting exercise at least at one of your meals today.

MORNING PROCESS

1. Contemplate the thought of the day.

2. **Practice New Thoughts:** let yourself cycle these thoughts. Write them out several

times and let yourself repeat them as you go on about your day. If new thoughts about your body come to you, add them to your daily list.

- I am confident that with practice I can tip the balance of my thoughts toward the support of what I'm wanting.
- It's fun to see just how much my thoughts affect and create my experience.
- It feels good to know that I can do something about my chronic thoughts.
- I like knowing that my body is most responsive to my thoughts.
- I like knowing that it's always been about my thoughts.

3. **Visualize/Day Dream:** What will it feel like when you reach your goal? What kind of clothes will you wear? Spend five minutes or so visualizing your new look. Feel the feelings. Picture yourself wearing something you've been wanting to wear. What will people say to you when they see you? What will you say to yourself when you look in the mirror?

EVENING PROCESS

1. Contemplate the thought of the day and record your feelings, insights, and reactions.

2. **Practice New Thoughts**

3. **Positive Focus:** Write 10 things you like about your body right now.

4. **Appreciate!** Appreciate! Appreciate!

Day 8

Thought of the day: you have total choice in how you see your body. You can choose to look at your body through the lens of appreciation and amazement or you can choose to look at your body through negative and critical eyes.

You can choose to see your body as thriving, capable, and resilient. You can choose to see your body as unlimited. You can choose to see your body as remarkable. You can choose to be in awe of your body and everything it does and is capable of doing.

It's a conscious choice and decision that you make in every moment.

Pre-meal Shifting: make an effort to do the Pre-meal Shifting excrcise at least at one of your meals today.

MORNING PROCESS

1. Contemplate the thought of the day.

2. **Practice New Thoughts:** let yourself cycle these thoughts. Write them out several times and let yourself repeat them as you go

on about your day. If new thoughts about your body come to you, add them to your daily list.

- The cells of my body are experts in their functioning.
- The conscious living cells of my body know exactly what they're doing.
- Every cell knows how to bring itself into balance.
- I'm going to allow my body to thrive today by thinking supportive thoughts.
- I'm going to trust and believe in my body's natural intelligence today.

3. **Visualize/Day Dream:** What will it feel like when you reach your goal? What kind of clothes will you wear? Spend five minutes or so visualizing your new look. Feel the feelings. Picture yourself wearing something you've been wanting to wear. What will people say to you when they see you? What will you say to yourself when you look in the mirror?

EVENING PROCESS

1. Contemplate the thought of the day and

record your feelings, insights, and reactions.

2. **Practice New Thoughts**

3. **Positive Focus:** Write 10 things you love about your body right now.

4. **Appreciate!** Appreciate! Appreciate!

Day 9

Thought of the day: your point of power for change is right now. It doesn't matter what you thought before this moment. It doesn't matter what thoughts you've practiced up until now because right here and right now you can create a change in your thought patterns. Right here and right now you can shift your consciousness. Your past practices are as relevant and significant as you make them. Your past experiences around weight are as relevant and significant as you make them in your Now. Right where you are today, right where you sit, you have total control in what aspects of your experience and in what thoughts you focus on. Right now is your new beginning. Right now is your fresh start. And you have the power to make this moment and what you decide within it the only relevant moment relative to your experiences with weight release.

Right here and right now is the only time and place in which you choose your thoughts. Now is all that matters! What thoughts are you choosing Now?

Pre-meal Shifting: make an effort to do the Pre-meal Shifting exercise at least at one of your meals today.

MORNING PROCESS

1. **Contemplate the thought of the day.**

2. **Practice New Thoughts:** let yourself cycle these thoughts. Write them out several times and let yourself repeat them as you go on about your day. If new thoughts about your body come to you, add them to your daily list.

   - What I thought about anything before this moment is as significant as I make it.
   - The beliefs I have practiced in the past are as relevant as I make them right now.
   - I now choose to form and shape my body through the thoughts and beliefs I choose now.
   - What thoughts I choose now is all that matters.
   - What thoughts I focus on now is all that affects my body from this moment on.

- I form my truths through the thoughts I practice.

3. **Visualize/Day Dream:** What will it feel like when you reach your goal? What kind of clothes will you wear? Visualize your new look. Feel the feelings. What will people say to you when they see you? What will you say to yourself when you look in the mirror?

EVENING PROCESS

1. Contemplate the thought of the day and record your feelings, insights, and reactions.

2. Practice New Thoughts

3. **Positive Focus:** Write 10 things you love about your body right now.

4. **Appreciate!** Appreciate! Appreciate!

Day 10

Thought of the day: when you learn to deliberately choose your thoughts and practice new better-feeling thoughts from day to day, you are literally re-setting the energetic mold that your cells conform to. And as you move through your day appreciating your body, loving your body, and continue to think good feeling thoughts about its ability and capability, you strengthen and solidify this mold. The only template or blueprint your body conforms to is created by the thoughts you have practiced. By deliberately choosing your thoughts, by deliberately training yourself to appreciate and celebrate the extraordinary nature of your body, you create the ideal foundation around which your *ideal* body builds itself.

Pre-meal Shifting: make an effort to do the Pre-meal Shifting exercise at least at one of your meals today.

MORNING PROCESS

1. Contemplate the thought of the day.

2. **Practice New Thoughts:** let yourself cycle
    these thoughts. Write them out several
    times and let yourself repeat them as you go
    on about your day. If new thoughts about
    your body come to you, add them to your
    daily list.

    - It feels so good to practice thoughts that
      support and celebrate my body.
    - My body is worth celebrating just as it is.
    - My body is amazing and magnificent in
      all that it does just as it is.
    - It feels good to appreciate my body.
    - It feels good to look at my body through
      a positive lens.

3. **Visualize/Day Dream:** What will it feel like
    when you reach your goal? What kind of
    clothes will you wear? Spend five minutes
    or so visualizing your new look. Feel the
    feelings. Picture yourself wearing something
    you've been wanting to wear. What will
    people say to you when they see you? What
    will you say to yourself when you look in
    the mirror?

EVENING PROCESS

1. Contemplate the thought of the day and record your feelings, insights, and reactions.

2. Practice New Thoughts

3. **Positive Focus:** Write 10 things you love about your body right now.

4. **Appreciate!** Appreciate! Appreciate!

Day 11

Thought of the day: pay attention to the story you've formed around your body, around weight, and around your ability to release that weight. What's on loop in your mind? What does the story sound like? What does the story feel like? What does the story say is possible? What does the story say is possible for you?

Recognize that every single truth you have about your body, is a thought you are practicing. Every belief you've formed, every fact you've formed in your mind, every conclusion you've made is just a thought you are practicing and continue to practice. And these practiced thoughts are the standards or expectations you've set for your body.

The mental story you tell about your body, about weight, and about your past experiences on this topic are the messages that you communicate to every single particle that is right now vibrating as your physical body. Your body cannot transcend the thought-limits you've set for it.

Make these thoughts known to yourself. Make these background narratives you have running on loop come into the foreground of your conscious awareness. In becoming aware of these stories you have running, and they are there running, from a place of non-judgement, you'll expose the faulty beliefs that have been running the show – you'll make the non-conscious beliefs stored in the subconscious and unconscious regions of your being fully conscious.

Pre-meal Shifting: make an effort to do the Pre-meal Shifting exercise at least at one of your meals today.

MORNING PROCESS

1. **Contemplate the thought of the day.**

2. **Practice New Thoughts:** let yourself cycle these thoughts. Write them out several times and let yourself repeat them as you go on about your day. If new thoughts about your body come to you, add them to your daily list.

   • The only limits are the ones I've set with my practiced thoughts.

- My body is unlimited.
- The intelligent particles of my body are unlimited in what they can do and in how they can be.

3. **Visualize/Day Dream:** What will it feel like when you reach your goal? What kind of clothes will you wear? Spend five minutes or so visualizing your new look. Feel the feelings. Picture yourself wearing something you've been wanting to wear. What will people say to you when they see you? What will you say to yourself when you look in the mirror?

EVENING PROCESS

1. Contemplate the thought of the day and record your feelings, insights, and reactions.

2. Practice New Thoughts

3. **Positive Focus:** Write 10 things you love about your body right now.

4. **Appreciate!** Appreciate! Appreciate!

Day 12

Thought of the day: you have accumulated thoughts around the subject of your body from all sorts of sources. Whether it is what you observed in your home growing up, what you heard from the media, what your doctors told you, what you learned in school, or whatever else, you have created many belief-sets that may or may not be serving you in any way.

The foremost authority of your body is not the outside world and the "experts" out there. It is your body itself. Your body is its own authority. Just as it had the intelligence to morph itself from a single cell into these trillions of cells each of whom have their own specificity and individual function, just as it effortlessly carries on numerous processes without the guidance and advice of the outside world of "experts", it can and does maintain its own wellbeing and longevity naturally through the guidance of its built-in intelligence.

There's nothing right or wrong about the information you have gathered thus far. What you have to ask yourself as you work to examine and shift your belief-sets is, "do these beliefs support the intelligence of my body or do they interfere with it?"

Pre-meal Shifting: make an effort to do the Pre-meal Shifting exercise at least at one of your meals today.

MORNING PROCESS

1. Contemplate the thought of the day.

2. Practice New Thoughts:

    - My body is the only expert on what it is capable of doing.
    - My body is as unlimited as I allow it to be.
    - My body itself has never needed outside information to function how it functions.
    - My body has never needed anyone to tell it how to flow blood or process oxygen or distribute nutrients or dispense energy.
    - I trust the intelligence of my body.

3. Visualize/Day Dream

EVENING PROCESS

1. Contemplate the thought of the day and record your feelings, insights, and reactions.
2. Practice New Thoughts
3. **Positive Focus:** Write 10 things you like about your body right now.
4. **Appreciate!** Appreciate! Appreciate!

Day 13

Thought of the day: your chronic thought patterns are at the heart of your every experience. No matter what you've tried or haven't tried, the success of your method is determined by the undercurrent of thoughts you have going on. When you work to shift these thought habits, you allow yourself and your chosen method to work for you at the most optimal level.

It's always about the balance of your thoughts, the mental grooves you have created.

Pre-meal Shifting: make an effort to do the Pre-meal Shifting exercise at least at one of your meals today.

MORNING PROCESS

1. Contemplate the thought of the day.

2. **Practice New Thoughts:** let yourself cycle these thoughts. Write them out several times and let yourself repeat them as you go on about your day. If new thoughts about your body come to you, add them to your daily list.

99

- Success is natural to me.
- With every good feeling thought I practice, I am letting my successful nature manifest.
- I'm focusing on my desired size and shape every day.
- I feel good about myself and my body.
- I know this works!

3. **Visualize/Day Dream:** What will it feel like when you reach your goal? What kind of clothes will you wear? Spend five minutes or so visualizing your new look. Feel the feelings. Picture yourself wearing something you've been wanting to wear. What will people say to you when they see you? What will you say to yourself when you look in the mirror?

EVENING PROCESS

1. Contemplate the thought of the day and record your feelings, insights, and reactions.

2. Practice New Thoughts

3. **Positive Focus:** Write 10 things you like

about your body right now.

4. **Appreciate!** Appreciate! Appreciate!

Day 14

Thought of the day: your natural state of being is one of absolute fulfillment. You were born to materialize and live out your desires. There is nothing that you cannot be, do, or have. There is nothing that you can't achieve or materialize. And as your body is immediate to all that your experience, the effect of your deliberate thinking will easily first be seen within it. You have unimaginable power. You can do the "impossible".

Pre-meal Shifting: make an effort to do the Pre-meal Shifting exercise at least at one of your meals today.

MORNING PROCESS

1. Contemplate the thought of the day.

2. Practice New Thoughts: let yourself cycle these thoughts. Write them out several times and let yourself repeat them as you go on about your day. If new thoughts about your body come to you, add them to your daily list.

- The cells of my body are unlimited in what they can achieve.
- The cells of my body have abilities and capabilities beyond my knowledge.
- The better I feel about my body, the more I allow myself to let in what I've asked for.
- Everything in my life exists to support the materialization of my desires.
- My desired size and shape is closer than I realize.

3. **Visualize/Day Dream:** What will it feel like when you reach your goal? What kind of clothes will you wear? Spend five minutes or so visualizing your new look. Feel the feelings. Picture yourself wearing something you've been wanting to wear. What will people say to you when they see you? What will you say to yourself when you look in the mirror?

EVENING PROCESS

1. Contemplate the thought of the day and record your feelings, insights, and reactions.

2. **Practice New Thoughts**

3. **Positive Focus:** Write 10 things you like about your body right now.

4. **Appreciate!** Appreciate! Appreciate!

Day 15

Thought of the day: the key is really to get out of the way and let your body do what you have asked of it to do. Your body absolutely responds to everything you ask of it. You have an ongoing dialogue with your body through your thoughts and emotions. So as you dwell on your desired size and shape and practice the good-feeling supportive thoughts, your body forms itself in the likeness of your request through your own inspiration and its own natural ability. Relax and allow it.

Pre-meal Shifting: make an effort to do the Pre-meal Shifting exercise at least at one of your meals today.

MORNING PROCESS

1. Contemplate the thought of the day.

2. **Practice New Thoughts:** let yourself cycle these thoughts. Write them out several times and let yourself repeat them as you go on about your day. If new thoughts about your body come to you, add them to your daily list.

- I am unleashing my power to change.
- I am exercising my intrinsic power.
- I now relax into my desired size and shape.
- I am enjoying and appreciating my body more and more each day.
- I am aware and appreciative of my supportive thoughts in each moment.

3. **Visualize/Day Dream:** What will it feel like when you reach your goal? What kind of clothes will you wear? Spend five minutes or so visualizing your new look. Feel the feelings. Picture yourself wearing something you've been wanting to wear. What will people say to you when they see you? What will you say to yourself when you look in the mirror?

EVENING PROCESS

1. Contemplate the thought of the day and record your feelings, insights, and reactions.

2. Practice New Thoughts

3. **Positive Focus:** Write 10 things you like about your body right now.

4. Appreciate! Appreciate! Appreciate!

Day 16

Thought of the day: motivation is different from inspiration. When you do something out of inspiration, your energy, the thoughts you have lined up are completely in sync with the activity you're setting out to do. There is an undercurrent of passion when you're acting from inspiration. There is energetic support when you're acting from inspiration. There is an invisible conspiracy of success when you're acting from inspiration.

When you're trying to motivate yourself on the other hand, you're in the moment trying to force yourself to move in a way that you haven't fully embraced or have come into alignment with. Motivation feels like you have to ramp up your energy whereas inspiration feels like you already have the energy. So inspired action energetically goes a long way further than motivated action.

Take the time to align with your chosen activity and method by dwelling on the positive aspects of it. As you do, you will naturally and spontaneously be moved toward that activity without an undercurrent of resistance or struggle. You don't have to force or hammer anything into place. You can make your movements and chosen activities a natural, enjoyable and fluid part of your daily life.

Pre-meal Shifting: make an effort to do the Pre-meal Shifting exercise at least at one of your meals today.

MORNING PROCESS

1. Contemplate the thought of the day.

2. **Practice New Thoughts:**

   - I am inspired when it comes to my body.
   - I can feel good about anything I do.
   - I can practice good feeling thoughts on whatever method of health and well-being I choose.
   - I can come into alignment with every activity I set out to do.
   - I can easily find inspiration.
   - I can easily be inspired to move in the way that allows me to achieve my goals.
   - Inspired actions come easily to me now and continuously.

3. **Visualize/Day Dream:** What will it feel like

when you reach your goal? What kind of clothes will you wear? Spend five minutes or so visualizing your new look. Feel the feelings. Picture yourself wearing something you've been wanting to wear. What will people say to you when they see you? What will you say to yourself when you look in the mirror?

EVENING PROCESS

1. Contemplate the thought of the day and record your feelings, insights, and reactions.

2. Practice New Thoughts

3. **Positive Focus:** Write 10 things you love about your body right now.

4. **Appreciate!** Appreciate! Appreciate!

Day 17

Thought of the day: your weight has never been about the food you eat or how much you move. Everything you put in your body is secondary. The primary digestion that takes place in your body is the digestion of your thoughts and emotions. Your body responds to everything you give to it within the boundaries of your beliefs. If you believe that you have to sweat and struggle to achieve your desired weight, your body conforms to that belief no matter what you do. If you believe that weight release is hard, then your body conforms to that belief no matter how hard you work. If you believe that there is good food and bad food, then your body conforms to that belief and reacts to and processes the food accordingly.

For every belief you hold, your body's answer is "your thought is my command". Your thoughts are the most powerful tools in your possession.

Pre-meal Shifting: make an effort to do the Pre-meal Shifting exercise at least at one of your meals today.

MORNING PROCESS

1. Contemplate the thought of the day.

2. Practice New Thoughts:

   - My thoughts are the most powerful tools that I have.
   - I am committed to thinking good feeling thoughts on the subject of my physical body.
   - I have choice in how I perceive, experience, and manifest my physical body.
   - It is more about energy than it is about biology or heredity.
   - I've always had the power to change and materialize my desired size and shape.

3. **Visualize/Day Dream:** What will it feel like when you reach your goal? What kind of clothes will you wear? Spend five minutes or so visualizing your new look. Feel the feelings. Picture yourself wearing something you've been wanting to wear. What will people say to you when they see you? What will you say to yourself when you look in the mirror?

EVENING PROCESS

1. Contemplate the thought of the day and record your feelings, insights, and reactions.

2. Practice New Thoughts

3. **Positive Focus:** Write 10 things you love about your body right now.

4. **Appreciate!** Appreciate! Appreciate!

Day 18

Thought of the day: focus on the activities that make you feel good, the one's you really enjoy. Whether it's dancing or walking or running, whatever it is, why do you enjoy it? Think about how these activities make you feel. Think about the feelings these activities generate within you. Take a moment to list them. Take a moment to consider what you like about them. Take a moment to just relish in how these activities stimulate and uplift you. What is the energy of the activities you enjoy? Now look at the thoughts you think about these activities and make note of their nature.

There is an absolute correlation between the activities you enjoy and the thoughts you think about these activities. You have the power to feel good about any activity you participate in by the simple selection and practice of deliberately chosen thoughts. There is no good or bad activity, there is only the thoughts you've practiced about that activity. It's all in the thoughts you've been practicing.

Pre-meal Shifting: make an effort to do the Pre-meal Shifting exercise at least at one of your meals today.

MORNING PROCESS

1. Contemplate the thought of the day.

2. Practice New Thoughts:

    - I can feel good about anything I choose.
    - I have absolute power of how I feel in any given activity.
    - I can enhance my level of enjoyment, and so the amount of energy that moves through me, by focusing on what I like about any activity.
    - I'm only limited by the thoughts I'm choosing to think.
    - My age, my size, my shape aren't the key players in my experience – my thoughts are always at the root of what I do and how I succeed in what I do.

3. **Visualize/Day Dream:** What will it feel like when you reach your goal? What kind of clothes will you wear? Spend five minutes or so visualizing your new look. Feel the feelings. Picture yourself wearing something you've been wanting to wear. What will people say to you when they see you? What

will you say to yourself when you look in the mirror?

EVENING PROCESS

1. Contemplate the thought of the day and record your feelings, insights, and reactions.

2. Practice New Thoughts

3. **Positive Focus:** Write 10 things you love about your body right now.

4. **Appreciate!** Appreciate! Appreciate!

Day 19

Thought of the day: Every behavior you engage in is as useful as your belief in it. It is your belief in your chosen weight release process that gets you results. If there was an outside condition that determined your success in meeting your goal, then everybody who ran on a treadmill every morning for 30 minutes should get the exact same results in the next seven days. But that's not how it unfolds. Not everybody gets the same results because not everyone is thinking the same types of thoughts. Not everyone is flowing their energy in support of their goal. Not everyone is allowing or resisting the flow of energy in the same way.

A positive belief, or a belief that supports your goal (i.c. "I love exercise. It really works well for me") will benefit your process much more so than a negative one. Any type of resistant thought, like "I hate running but I have to do it", is actually working against your goal. As you're thinking negative thoughts while engaging in things you "have" to do, you're disallowing the flow of the energy that creates and recreates your body and so resisting the very results that you have asked for.

The formula is simple. Positive or good-feeling thoughts allow your desire to manifest. Negative or bad-feeling thoughts disallow the materialization of your goals. Back-up whatever process or method you've concluded works best for you by practicing positive or good feeling thoughts about that method.

Pre-meal Shifting: make an effort to do the Pre-meal Shifting exercise at least at one of your meals today.

MORNING PROCESS

1. Contemplate the thought of the day.

2. Practice New Thoughts:

- I am aware of the types of thoughts I'm thinking.
- I am thinking thoughts in support of my goal.
- I consciously appreciate the processes I've chosen as my tools for weight release.
- I deliberately think positive thoughts about my chosen tools for weight

release.

- I choose for my mantra to be "this is working for me, this is working for me, this is supporting me."

3. **Visualize/Day Dream:** What will it feel like when you reach your goal? What kind of clothes will you wear? What will people say to you when they see you? What will you say to yourself when you look in the mirror?

EVENING PROCESS

1. Contemplate the thought of the day and record your feelings, insights, and reactions.

2. Practice New Thoughts

3. **Positive Focus:** Write 10 things you love about your body right now.

4. **Appreciate! Appreciate! Appreciate!**

Day 20

Thought of the day: you didn't get to where you are overnight. Meaning there have been a lot of little thoughts you've practiced along the way that have built up the patterns you are now deliberately shifting.

Be patient with yourself. Be your own champion and cheerleader. Encourage yourself every step of the way and recognize that your efforts are doing much more than you may be able to immediately visibly realize. Appreciate your efforts. Your own self-appreciation is a part of the shifting process.

Pre-meal Shifting: make an effort to do the Pre-meal Shifting exercise at least at one of your meals today.

MORNING PROCESS

1. Contemplate the thought of the day.

2. Practice New Thoughts: let yourself cycle these thoughts. Write them out several times and let yourself repeat them as you go on about your day. If new thoughts about

your body come to you, add them to your
daily list.

- I'm doing really well.
- I'm doing so much better than I realize.
- I'm really getting the hang of this.
- My feeling better in any moment is
  telling me that I'm right on track.
- I'm getting this right.

3. **Visualize/Day Dream:** What will it feel like
   when you reach your goal? What kind of
   clothes will you wear? Spend five minutes
   or so visualizing your new look. Feel the
   feelings. Picture yourself wearing something
   you've been wanting to wear. What will
   people say to you when they see you? What
   will you say to yourself when you look in
   the mirror?

EVENING PROCESS

1. Contemplate the thought of the day and
   record your feelings, insights, and reactions.

2. **Practice New Thoughts**

3. **Positive Focus:** Write 10 things you like

about your body right now.

4. **Appreciate!** Appreciate! Appreciate!

Day 21

Thought of the day: there is no difference mentally between what you perceive to be real and what you perceive to be a thought you are deliberately choosing. The "reality" of your body, the way you mentally conceive of it, is still a thought that you are thinking. Whether you look at your body and think "my hips are big" or "I look fabulous" these are thoughts you are thinking. They're both just thoughts. They're both just mental evaluations. What makes one feel truer than the other is how often you have practiced that thought – how much power you have supplied to that thought. Every thought you believe is your reality only appears so because of the amount of power you've been applying and supplying to it. And since your body responds to whatever thought you practice, your change in thoughts will soon be followed with manifestation. Your desired results are inevitable.

Pre-meal Shifting: make an effort to do the Pre-meal Shifting exercise at least at one of your meals today.

MORNING PROCESS

1. **Contemplate the thought of the day.**

2. **Practice New Thoughts:** let yourself cycle these thoughts. Write them out several times and let yourself repeat them as you go on about your day. If new thoughts about your body come to you, add them to your daily list.

    - My body is good to me.
    - I support my body's well-being through the thoughts I think.
    - My body is amazing.
    - My body is extraordinary in every way.
    - I love and appreciate my body.

3. **Visualize/Day Dream:** What will it feel like when you reach your goal? What kind of clothes will you wear? Spend five minutes or so visualizing your new look. Feel the feelings. Picture yourself wearing something you've been wanting to wear. What will people say to you when they see you? What will you say to yourself when you look in the mirror?

EVENING PROCESS

1. Contemplate the thought of the day and record your feelings, insights, and reactions.

2. Practice New Thoughts

3. **Positive Focus:** Write 10 things you like about your body right now.

4. **Appreciate!** Appreciate! Appreciate!

Day 22

Thought of the day: every person that you come across looks and feels as they do because of the quality of their thoughts – the subtle story in their mind that's constantly being played. There is no other builder of this physical experience. The root of everything you see, the foundational basis is a thought – a subtle form of energy that you translate into thought then into physical experience.

Pre-meal Shifting: make an effort to do the Pre-meal Shifting exercise at least at one of your meals today.

MORNING PROCESS

1. Contemplate the thought of the day.

2. **Practice New Thoughts:** let yourself cycle these thoughts. Write them out several times and let yourself repeat them as you go on about your day. If new thoughts about your body come to you, add them to your daily list.

    • All I ever experience is the effect of my

thoughts.
- My body is an outcome of the thoughts I've been thinking.
- As I choose better feeling thoughts, a better feeling body is certain to follow.

3. **Visualize/Day Dream:** What will it feel like when you reach your goal? What kind of clothes will you wear? Spend five minutes or so visualizing your new look. Feel the feelings. Picture yourself wearing something you've been wanting to wear. What will people say to you when they see you? What will you say to yourself when you look in the mirror?

EVENING PROCESS

1. **Contemplate the thought of the day and record your feelings, insights, and reactions.**

2. **Practice New Thoughts**

3. **Positive Focus:** Write 10 things you like about your body right now.

4. **Appreciate!** Appreciate! Appreciate!

Day 23

Thought of the day: the cells of your body already know what they need and what to do to be what you have asked them to be. You just have to get out of your own way by not introducing contradictory information through your old habits of thought.

Anytime you ask your body for a physical change, anytime you acknowledge or have a preference about how you want your body to look and feel, and then think thoughts in opposition to this requested change, anytime you think thoughts that oppose the manifestation of your desire, you are interfering with your cells natural ability to morph into the body you want.

Your only work is really to think thoughts that allow what you are wanting. The cells, the intelligence of your body will do everything else. You will crave the right foods. You will crave the right movements. You will naturally move with the flow of your desire rather than against it.

Pre-meal Shifting: make an effort to do the Pre-meal Shifting exercise at least at one of your meals today.

MORNING PROCESS

1. Contemplate the thought of the day.

2. Practice New Thoughts:

   - I am aware of what types of thoughts I am thinking.
   - All I have to do is find good-feeling thoughts.
   - My body naturally knows what it needs and what to do.
   - I support and love my body.
   - I trust my body's innate intelligence.

3. Visualize/Day Dream

EVENING PROCESS

1. Contemplate the thought of the day and record your feelings, insights, and reactions.

2. Practice New Thoughts

3. **Positive Focus:** Write 10 things you like about your body right now.

4. Appreciate! Appreciate! Appreciate!

Day 24

Thought of the day: with every critical thought you have about the way your body looks or feels, you are deciding the formation of your body. Every thought is responded to. Every time.

"I am fat" will get you just that. "I have a hard time losing weight" will get you just that. "It's hard to keep the weight off" will get you just that. "I'm too lazy for all that hard work" will get you just that. "I really shouldn't be eating this" will get you exactly the kind of result you think it'll get you. Everything is conforming to the thoughts you're practicing.

Pre-meal Shifting: make an effort to do the Pre-meal Shifting exercise at least at one of your meals today.

MORNING PROCESS

1. Contemplate the thought of the day.

2. **Practice New Thoughts:** let yourself cycle these thoughts. Write them out several times and let yourself repeat them as you go on about your day. If new thoughts about

your body come to you, add them to your
daily list.

- This is easy, because my body knows
  exactly what it's doing.
- It's all about the thoughts I have
  practiced.
- This is as easy as I think it will be.
- My thoughts are all that determine the
  outcome.
- My body is an out-picturing of the
  thoughts I have lined up.

3. **Visualize/Day Dream:** What will it feel like
   when you reach your goal? What kind of
   clothes will you wear? Spend five minutes
   or so visualizing your new look. Feel the
   feelings. Picture yourself wearing something
   you've been wanting to wear. What will
   people say to you when they see you? What
   will you say to yourself when you look in
   the mirror?

EVENING PROCESS

1. Contemplate the thought of the day and
   record your feelings, insights, and reactions.

2. **Practice New Thoughts**

3. **Positive Focus:** Write 10 things you like about your body right now.

4. **Appreciate!** Appreciate! Appreciate!

Day 25

Thought of the day: you can train your mind toward positive anticipation and expectation on any subject. You can practice thoughts of positive expectation and habituate a thought pattern that is supportive of the materialization of your desire. And as you do, as you anchor and encode your being with the energy of positive thoughts, your desired manifestation is certain. You will always easily get what you expect to get.

Pre-meal Shifting: make an effort to do the Pre-meal Shifting exercise at least at one of your meals today.

MORNING PROCESS

1. Contemplate the thought of the day.

2. **Practice New Thoughts:** let yourself cycle these positive-anticipatory thoughts. Write them out several times and let yourself repeat them as you go on about your day. If new thoughts about your body come to you, add them to your daily list.

- This really was never about hard work.
- What if the weight just came off?
- What if it's all so effortless and easy?
- What if people start noticing how I'm physically changing?
- What if I can fit into a size ____ tomorrow?
- What if I'm already changing in the best possible way?

3. **Visualize/Day Dream:** What will it feel like when you reach your goal? What kind of clothes will you wear? Spend five minutes or so visualizing your new look. Feel the feelings. Picture yourself wearing something you've been wanting to wear. What will people say to you when they see you? What will you say to yourself when you look in the mirror?

EVENING PROCESS

1. Contemplate the thought of the day and record your feelings, insights, and reactions.

2. Practice New Thoughts

3. **Positive Focus:** Write 10 things you like about your body right now.

4. **Appreciate!** Appreciate! Appreciate!

Day 26

Thought of the day: it does not serve you to dwell on what thoughts you may have practiced in the past or what negative patterns you catch yourself entertaining as you're going through this deliberate shift.

Your point of absolute power is in your Now-moment. The only place is here, and the only time is now, so all that matters is the thoughts you're choosing to focus on <u>right now</u>. Lift off of any tendency that takes you into self-criticalness or guilt or any other negative feeling over past efforts and actions. The past is only a story you tell in your mind. The past is only a thought you're thinking in your Now-moment.

The only thing that serves you in the materialization of your desires, is to think thoughts that feel good, to think thoughts that are in line with your chosen goal – and you choose those thoughts right here and right now.

Pre-meal Shifting: make an effort to do the Prc-meal Shifting exercise at least at one of your meals today.

MORNING PROCESS

1. Contemplate the thought of the day.

2. Practice New Thoughts:

   - I am doing so well.
   - I'm right on track.
   - I'm getting all of this.
   - I feel good about my efforts.
   - I so appreciate myself for choosing to deliberately exercise my power.

3. **Visualize/Day Dream:** What will it feel like when you reach your goal? What kind of clothes will you wear? Spend five minutes or so visualizing your new look. Feel the feelings. Picture yourself wearing something you've been wanting to wear. What will people say to you when they see you? What will you say to yourself when you look in the mirror?

EVENING PROCESS

1. Contemplate the thought of the day and record your feelings, insights, and reactions.

2. **Practice New Thoughts**

3. **Positive Focus:** Write 10 things you like about your body right now.

4. **Appreciate!** Appreciate! Appreciate!

Day 27

Thought of the day: anything you tell yourself is "bad" for you will be. Anything you say "will go straight to my hips" will do just that. Your body is responding to your beliefs and behaving within the boundaries you've set. Everything you eat will do exactly what you expect it to do. Every movement you make will do exactly what you expect it to do.

Pay attention to your expectations, the thoughts that you've practiced on the food groups you consume, the diets you take part in, and the exercise programs you engage in. It's not about what the food will do to your body. It's not about what the diets will do to your body. It's not about what the work-outs will do to your body. It's about what you believe the food, the diets, the exercises will do to your body. Everything is about your beliefs.

Pre-meal Shifting: make an effort to do the Pre-meal Shifting exercise at least at one of your meals today.

MORNING PROCESS

1. Contemplate the thought of the day.

153

2. **Practice New Thoughts:** let yourself cycle these thoughts. Write them out several times and let yourself repeat them as you go on about your day. If new thoughts about your body come to you, add them to your daily list.

- My food is satisfying.
- My food is a pleasurable experience.
- My food brings me a sense of well-being.
- My food satisfies me in healthy ways!
- The foods I choose really fuel and energize me!
- My body easily releases whatever it doesn't need as fuel.

3. **Visualize/Day Dream:** What will it feel like when you reach your goal? What kind of clothes will you wear? Spend five minutes or so visualizing your new look. Feel the feelings. Picture yourself wearing something you've been wanting to wear. What will people say to you when they see you? What will you say to yourself when you look in the mirror?

EVENING PROCESS

1. Contemplate the thought of the day and record your feelings, insights, and reactions.

2. Practice New Thoughts

3. **Positive Focus:** Write 10 things you like about your body right now.

4. **Appreciate!** Appreciate! Appreciate!

Day 28

Thought of the day: whatever you resist, you actually supply and add more power to. Whatever you resist will in fact persist. If there is anything about your physicality that you are resisting, it will stick around. Whether your attention on any aspect of yourself is positive or negative, you are by the very act of paying attention to it adding more power to the reality of it.

As you deliberately shift your thoughts toward the love and appreciation of your various physical aspects, you stop supplying the power of your life-giving attention into what it is you do not want. You stop supplying and applying your power, your all-nourishing attention, to what is unwanted.

Your body becomes what you think of it most often. When you see it with love and appreciation as it is right now, it will become even more of the physical system you can love and appreciate.

Pre-meal Shifting: make an effort to do the Pre-meal Shifting exercise at least at one of your meals today.

MORNING PROCESS

1. Contemplate the thought of the day.

2. **Practice New Thoughts:** let yourself cycle these thoughts. Write them out several times and let yourself repeat them as you go on about your day. If new thoughts about your body come to you, add them to your daily list.

   - I love every aspect of my body.
   - I welcome and accept every part of my body just as it is.
   - My body is beautiful and amazing just as it is.
   - My body does more things for me effortlessly than I ever realized before.
   - My body is such a wonderful gift.

3. Visualize/Day Dream

EVENING PROCESS

1. Contemplate the thought of the day and record your feelings, insights, and reactions.

2. **Practice New Thoughts**

3. **Positive Focus:** Write 10 things you like about your body right now.

4. **Appreciate!** Appreciate! Appreciate!

Day 29

Thought of the day: everything in your life will conspire to bring to you the balance of your thinking – the essence of your practiced and frequent thoughts. When you deliberately and consistently give your attention to thoughts that are appreciating and loving your body, when you deliberately and consistently choose thoughts that are telling it and describing it the way you want it to be, everything in your life will shift to mirror the powerful thoughts you now have about your body – to materialize that body into your reality.

The conditions to materialize your desired appearance will reveal themselves. Change your mind, and you absolutely and completely change your body for the long term.

Pre-meal Shifting: make an effort to do the Pre-meal Shifting exercise at least at one of your meals today.

MORNING PROCESS

1. Contemplate the thought of the day.

2. **Practice New Thoughts:** let yourself cycle these thoughts. Write them out several times and let yourself repeat them as you go on about your day. If new thoughts about your body come to you, add them to your daily list.

- My body reflects the balance of my thoughts.
- I have absolute choice in how my body appears.
- The more I practice thoughts that feel better, the better I get at it.
- My body is doing really well and so am I.

3. **Visualize/Day Dream**

EVENING PROCESS

1. Contemplate the thought of the day and record your feelings, insights, and reactions.

2. Practice New Thoughts

3. **Positive Focus:** Write 10 new things you

love about your body right now.

4. **Appreciate!** Appreciate! Appreciate!

Day 30

Thought of the day: start seeing what a brilliant organized system your body truly is. Start seeing your body through the eyes of awe and amazement instead of the eyes of criticism and judgment. Start seeing just how much about your body is working right, is functioning flawlessly right in this moment. Let your mind linger on the inexplicable brilliance of your body's ability to do everything that it does with no conscious thought and input on your part. Practice seeing your body through this kind of a lens, through these kinds of thoughts. As you do, your body will continue to awe and amaze you in new ways.

Pre-meal Shifting: make an effort to do the Pre-meal Shifting exercise at least at one of your meals today.

MORNING PROCESS

1. Contemplate the thought of the day.

2. **Practice New Thoughts:** let yourself cycle these thoughts. Write them out several times and let yourself repeat them as you go

165

on about your day. If new thoughts about your body come to you, add them to your daily list.

- My body is more brilliant than I ever thought it to be.
- I love seeing my body through eyes of amazement.
- I love seeing my body through eyes of awe.
- My body deserves my love and appreciation.

3. **Visualize/Day Dream:** What does it feel like when you reach your goal? What kind of clothes do you wear? Spend five minutes or so visualizing your new look. Feel the feelings. Picture yourself wearing something you've been wanting to wear. What do people say to you when they see you? What do you say to yourself when you look in the mirror?

EVENING PROCESS

1. Contemplate the thought of the day and record your feelings, insights, and reactions.

2. **Practice New Thoughts**

3. **Positive Focus:** Write 10 things you like about your body right now.

4. **Appreciate!** Appreciate! Appreciate!

Day 31

Thought of the day: change your mind about what you think you see as your body. Everything you see, you see through the filter of your thoughts. You can look at your body through a positive lens, through a lineup of good feeling thoughts, or you can look at your body through a negative lens, through a lineup of critical and "bad" feeling thoughts. It makes a significant difference to your experience and outcome which lens you choose.

Everything you perceive is actually an interpretation of the vibrations around you. What you see as your body is an interpretation of the energy or frequency you've lined up. What do you think your eyes are registering? What do you think your sense of touch is registering? It is all a translation of energy in motion. Your senses are registering external stimuli that your brain then translates into electrical information.

Every thought you entertain, whether it is a thought of "reality" or a thought of "imagination" is registered by your brain in the same way. Your brain doesn't distinguish between reality and imagination. The universe doesn't distinguish between reality and imagination. So it makes all the difference what thoughts you are encoding your being with. It makes all the difference what it is that you've taught yourself to see. And you can train yourself to see anything!

Pre-meal Shifting: make an effort to do warm-up to your food at least at one of your meals today.

MORNING PROCESS

1. Contemplate the thought of the day.

2. Practice New Thoughts

- I choose to focus on the positive aspects of my body.
- I choose to see and experience my body from a positive perspective.
- I choose to praise my body and appearance.

3. Visualize/Day Dream

EVENING PROCESS

1. Contemplate the thought of the day and record your feelings, insights, and reactions.

2. Practice New Thoughts

3. **Positive Focus:** Write 10 things you like about your body right now.

4. **Appreciate!** Appreciate! Appreciate!

Day 32

Thought of the day: the vibrating particles that make up your body are forming themselves in accord to the template of your cemented beliefs. Your beliefs, or mental programming, are the driving power of why your body looks and feels the way it does. Your beliefs about and around your body and weight, or your Weight Consciousness as it were, are the most powerful determinants of your physical appearance and make-up. Reconfigure your Weight Consciousness, and you will see that change materialize.

Pre-meal Shifting: make an effort to do the Pre-meal Shifting exercise at least at one of your meals today.

MORNING PROCESS

1. Contemplate the thought of the day.

2. **Practice New Thoughts:** let yourself cycle these thoughts. Write them out several times and let yourself repeat them as you go on about your day. If new thoughts about your body come to you, add them to your

daily list.

- I am becoming more and more aware of the story around my weight and appearance.
- I am consciously changing my root beliefs around my weight.
- The root cause of my weight and appearance is the thoughts I have been practicing up until now.

3. **Visualize/Day Dream:** What does it feel like when you reach your goal? What kind of clothes do you wear? Spend five minutes or so visualizing your new look. Feel the feelings. Picture yourself wearing something you've been wanting to wear. What do people say to you when they see you? What do you say to yourself when you look in the mirror?

EVENING PROCESS

1. Contemplate the thought of the day and record your feelings, insights, and reactions.

2. Practice New Thoughts

3. **Positive Focus:** Write 10 things you like about your body right now.

4. **Appreciate!** Appreciate! Appreciate!

Day 33

Thought of the day: the only limitations you have, are the ones you believe you have. The only limitations there are, are only the one's you've practiced into being. The only limits there are to what you can do, to what your body can do, are the limits you have set up by your practiced patterns of thought, your beliefs and conclusions.

Pre-meal Shifting: make an effort to do the Pre-meal Shifting exercise at least at one of your meals today.

MORNING PROCESS

1. **Contemplate the thought of the day.**

2. **Practice New Thoughts:** let yourself cycle these thoughts. Write them out several times and let yourself repeat them as you go on about your day. If new thoughts about your body come to you, add them to your daily list.

   • I am as unlimited as I believe myself to be.

177

- My goals are as possible as I believe them to be.
- There are no limits to what my body can become.

3. **Visualize/Day Dream:** What does it feel like when you reach your goal? What kind of clothes do you wear? Spend five minutes or so visualizing your new look. Feel the feelings. Picture yourself wearing something you've been wanting to wear. What do people say to you when they see you? What do you say to yourself when you look in the mirror?

EVENING PROCESS

1. Contemplate the thought of the day and record your feelings, insights, and reactions.

2. Practice New Thoughts

3. **Positive Focus:** Write 10 things you like about your body right now.

4. **Appreciate!** Appreciate! Appreciate!

Day 34

Thought of the day: break your practiced patterns of thought, your automatic story, through deliberate effort. As you change your root ideas of what your body is, why it looks the way it does, and what it can do, you will see the change in these root ideas materialize as your experience. Your thoughts are at the source of everything you experience.

Pre-meal Shifting: make an effort to do the Pre-meal Shifting exercise at least at one of your meals today.

MORNING PROCESS

1. Contemplate the thought of the day.

2. **Practice New Thoughts:** let yourself cycle these thoughts. Write them out several times and let yourself repeat them as you go on about your day. If new thoughts about your body come to you, add them to your daily list.

   - I am unlimited.
   - I have more power to bring forth change

than I have ever realized.

- Biology and heredity are secondary to my Weight Consciousness, to the story I tell.
- The thoughts I practice are at the root of everything I experience.
- I have more control than I ever realized.

3. **Visualize/Day Dream:** What does it feel like when you reach your goal? What kind of clothes do you wear? Spend five minutes or so visualizing your new look. Feel the feelings. Picture yourself wearing something you've been wanting to wear. What do people say to you when they see you? What do you say to yourself when you look in the mirror?

EVENING PROCESS

1. Contemplate the thought of the day and record your feelings, insights, and reactions.

2. Practice New Thoughts

3. **Positive Focus:** Write 10 things you like about your body right now.

4. Appreciate! Appreciate! Appreciate!

Day 35

Thought of the day: everything you have ever learned about what your body can do and what your body needs are just ideas one person had and then materialized into physical evidence. Everything you believe about your body is someone else's idea you've incorporated into your base program, or foundational blueprint. It is neither good nor bad, but it is still just someone else's idea, it is still how someone else has flown their energy and materialized physical evidence.

Pre-meal Shifting: make an effort to do the Pre-meal Shifting exercise at least at one of your meals today.

MORNING PROCESS

1. Contemplate the thought of the day.

2. **Practice New Thoughts:** let yourself cycle these thoughts. Write them out several times and let yourself repeat them as you go on about your day. If new thoughts about your body come to you, add them to your daily list.

183

- I can create my body from my own ideas of what I can be and what it can do.
- I can create a body based on unlimited ideas.
- I can allow my body's full potential to materialize.
- I am the owner of the ideas I materialize and so I have full power in what changes I allow.

3. **Visualize/Day Dream:** What does it feel like when you reach your goal? What kind of clothes do you wear? Spend five minutes or so visualizing your new look. Feel the feelings. Picture yourself wearing something you've been wanting to wear. What do people say to you when they see you? What do you say to yourself when you look in the mirror?

EVENING PROCESS

1. Contemplate the thought of the day and record your feelings, insights, and reactions.

2. **Practice New Thoughts**

3. **Positive Focus:** Write 10 things you like about your body right now.

4. **Appreciate!** Appreciate! Appreciate!

Day 36

Thought of the day: you are much more a system of light waves, or energy packets in constant communication, than you are a system of solid fixed unchanging matter. You are much more energy and particles in continuous movement than you are a gathering of solid bones and fluids. Consider looking at your idea of being a "physical being". What does that mean? What is "physical"? What is your body really made of? And how absolutely fluid and malleable is it?

Pre-meal Shifting: make an effort to do the Pre-meal Shifting exercise at least at one of your meals today.

MORNING PROCESS

1. Contemplate the thought of the day.

2. **Practice New Thoughts:** let yourself cycle these thoughts. Write them out several times and let yourself repeat them as you go on about your day. If new thoughts about your body come to you, add them to your daily list.

187

- My body is much more malleable than I ever considered.
- My body is made of particles that are in constant motion.
- My body is much more changeable than I ever realized.
- My body is much more flexible than I ever thought possible.

3. **Visualize/Day Dream:** What does it feel like when you reach your goal? What kind of clothes do you wear? Spend five minutes or so visualizing your new look. Feel the feelings. Picture yourself wearing something you've been wanting to wear. What do people say to you when they see you? What do you say to yourself when you look in the mirror?

EVENING PROCESS

1. Contemplate the thought of the day and record your feelings, insights, and reactions.

2. Practice New Thoughts

3. **Positive Focus:** Write 10 things you like about your body right now.

4. **Appreciate!** Appreciate! Appreciate!

Day 37

Thought of the day: bring to your conscious awareness what your programmed beliefs around weight are. What makes you gain or lose weight? What do you believe you're capable of looking like? What do you believe it will take to look and feel how you want to look and feel?

Think of all your possible answers and then recognize that all of your answers are changeable practiced patterns of thought. They are beliefs you've either picked up in this physical experience or have trained yourself into forming. They are thoughts you've practiced in your lifetime. They are thoughts you've made real for yourself through the years. And because they are thoughts you've practiced, you can change them.

Recognize that it is much easier than your practiced patterns of thought can right now allow you to realize.

Pre-meal Shifting: make an effort to do the Pre-meal Shifting exercise at least at one of your meals today.

MORNING PROCESS

1. Contemplate the thought of the day.

2. **Practice New Thoughts:** let yourself cycle these thoughts. Write them out several times and let yourself repeat them as you go on about your day. If new thoughts about your body come to you, add them to your daily list.

    - My body's ability to transform itself is easier than I ever thought possible.
    - My body's ability to utilize the energy from what I eat is more tremendous than I ever conceived.
    - There's so much more to what my body can do than I ever realized.
    - I love knowing that the only thing that determines the outcome of my physical body are the thoughts I have habituated.

3. Visualize/Day Dream

EVENING PROCESS

1. Contemplate the thought of the day and

record your feelings, insights, and reactions.

2. **Practice New Thoughts**

3. **Positive Focus:** Write 10 things you love about your body right now.

4. **Appreciate!** Appreciate! Appreciate!

Day 38

Thought of the day: the energy stream that makes up your body and everything around you has the unlimited capability of forming itself into anything desired. Just take a look at everything around you and within you and recognize that it is one energy stream forming itself into these infinite patterns before you. Everything about you is unlimited in every sense of the word. That unequivocally includes your body.

Pre-meal Shifting: make an effort to do the Pre-meal Shifting exercise at least at one of your meals today.

MORNING PROCESS

1. Contemplate the thought of the day.

2. **Practice New Thoughts:** let yourself cycle these thoughts. Write them out several times and let yourself repeat them as you go on about your day. If new thoughts about your body come to you, add them to your daily list.

- The energy that materializes as my body is capable of anything.
- The energy stream that makes up my body is unlimited.
- The energy stream that builds my body can form itself into anything I can imagine.
- I am unlimited in every sense of the word.

3. **Visualize/Day Dream:** What does it feel like when you reach your goal? What kind of clothes do you wear? Spend five minutes or so visualizing your new look. Feel the feelings. Picture yourself wearing something you've been wanting to wear. What do people say to you when they see you? What do you say to yourself when you look in the mirror?

EVENING PROCESS

1. Contemplate the thought of the day and record your feelings, insights, and reactions.

2. Practice New Thoughts

3. **Positive Focus:** Write 10 things you like about your body right now.

4. **Appreciate!** Appreciate! Appreciate!

Day 39

Thought of the day: the particles that make up your body have their own innate intelligence and reason for being. Every cell, every particle that makes up your body is well aware of what it is here to do and function as. Your skin cells know their function. Your hair cells know their function. Your heart cells know their function. Every particle that has materialized as a cell in your body knows exactly what it is here to do. And every one of these trillions of cells, every one of these particles that make up your body obey your desires skillfully. Every particle of your body is absolutely and masterfully responsive to your intentions and attention.

Pre-meal Shifting: make an effort to do the Pre-meal Shifting exercise at least at one of your meals today.

MORNING PROCESS

1. Contemplate the thought of the day.

2. **Practice New Thoughts:** let yourself cycle these thoughts. Write them out several

times and let yourself repeat them as you go on about your day. If new thoughts about your body come to you, add them to your daily list.

- The particles of my body are constantly receiving instruction from me.
- The particles that make up my body are obedient to my every request.
- The particles that make up my body are skillfully responsive to my intention and attention.
- My body is a co-creation between my thoughts and the energy that forms my body.

3. **Visualize/Day Dream:** What does it feel like when you reach your goal? What kind of clothes do you wear? Spend five minutes or so visualizing your new look. Feel the feelings. Picture yourself wearing something you've been wanting to wear. What do people say to you when they see you? What do you say to yourself when you look in the mirror?

EVENING PROCESS

1. Contemplate the thought of the day and record your feelings, insights, and reactions.

2. Practice New Thoughts

3. **Positive Focus:** Write 10 things you like about your body right now.

4. **Appreciate!** Appreciate! Appreciate!

Day 40

Thought of the day: you really aren't a physical human with a fixed and unchanging weight. You really are not a gathering of hard matter weighing more or less than you want to weigh. You are a system of vibrations, packets of energy that are in constant motion, who has practiced looking at the body through a line-up of specific thoughts, thoughts that cannot show you just how malleable and changeable everything in your view truly is.

Change this lens, the line-up of thoughts you have practiced, and you will not only feel how unlimited you are but you will see your limitlessness materialize as the body of your dreams.

Pre-meal Shifting: make an effort to do the Pre-meal Shifting exercise at least at one of your meals today.

MORNING PROCESS

1. Contemplate the thought of the day.

2. **Practice New Thoughts:** let yourself cycle these thoughts. Write them out several

times and let yourself repeat them as you go on about your day. If new thoughts about your body come to you, add them to your daily list.

- I am a vibrational being in every sense of the word.
- There is nothing solid or fixed about my body.
- My body is energy in constant motion.
- My food is energy in constant motion.
- Everything about me is in constant and rapid movement.

3. **Visualize/Day Dream:** What does it feel like when you reach your goal? What kind of clothes do you wear? Spend five minutes or so visualizing your new look. Feel the feelings. Picture yourself wearing something you've been wanting to wear. What do people say to you when they see you? What do you say to yourself when you look in the mirror?

EVENING PROCESS

1. Contemplate the thought of the day and record your feelings, insights, and reactions.

2. **Practice New Thoughts**

3. **Positive Focus:** Write 10 things you like about your body right now.

4. **Appreciate!** Appreciate! Appreciate!

PART III

Your New Template

Your practiced pattern of thought, the story that plays out in your mind, on every subject is everything that you experience. Until there is a change in that story, until there is a shift in the story you tell yourself about what your body is or what it can do, whatever change you force on the surface will disintegrate before your eyes. This is why most of the programs available to people don't work. Your unchanged mind, your consciousness will always come through and materialize in some way.

Any change that occurs on the surface level of your physical being, any success you gain and allow without changing the root cause of your experience does not last. An old falling house with new paint will still fall. There's nothing rooted to hold that superficial change in place. The structure is still unsound. Your blueprint and foundation is still the same, it has not changed. The change must come from within as a shift in your very outlook and understanding of what your body is, and what it can do.

It isn't about diets. It isn't about exercises. It isn't about struggle. It isn't about sweat. It isn't about labor. It isn't about anything you've taught yourself it's about because all of those premises are founded upon the notion that your body is a solid clump of "stuff". It isn't about anything that you do on the physical level. Consciousness, energy, particles vibrating at speeds invisible to your senses is what makes up your seemingly physical experience. Perceive and experience the change from this level of perception and you will step into an empowered unfailing system of lasting change.

The exercises and thoughts contained in this text are allowing you to shape a new story, create a new vibrational template, within yourself. This new story is everything. This new story is your building block. This new story and understanding, this new shift in how you experience your physical system and world from moment to moment, is what determines what and how you now predominately think, what you predominately say, and what you do.

Your entire pattern of motivation is altered. You are altering the very structure of how you move through your moments. This story is what determines what energy you constantly radiate or emanate outward on every level of your being. This new pattern is what determines the spin of the particles that make up your physical body. This new story is what determines how you experience your physical body and what this body materializes itself into. All things grow out of your practiced habits of thought, the very energies you're constantly encoding your entire being with.

Every single behavior that you take part in, every word you speak, every compulsion you experience yourself having, every motivation you find yourself experiencing, is an effect of the thoughts you have been practicing. The root of all that you experience and express is the silent story you have within yourself, the story on loop in your mind. When the story in your mind shifts to be about your unlimited nature in every aspect of your being, everything about you from your body outward will shift to materialize or mirror this internal expansion, this internal shift in your consciousness that you have deliberately brought forth.

You are no longer working with the effects or the outcomes of your thoughts. You are no longer working with the conditions and circumstances materializing out of your thoughts. You are working with the root cause itself. You are working with the foundation. You are working with the template, the blueprint. You are creating permanent change in your consciousness. And you are doing this steadily, consistently, and gently.

Can you think yourself slim? Can you think yourself into the body you've dreamed of?

Your criteria for weight release are only thoughts you have practiced. You're the only one that can decide what you can and cannot do. You're the only one that can determine what your body is capable of, and what you yourself are capable of, through the belief-sets or rule-sets you've set up for yourself. You create what you believe. You live out the expectations you have formed. You decide.

Acknowledge yourself every step of the way and commit to creating the change from the inside out. A change of that nature will be irreversible because you will be standing solidly in your power to bring about whatever you desire into your reality through YOUR power of focus. Mind your mind. Pay attention to the inputs you validate and integrate into your own consciousness. Be firm and steady in your commitment to yourself to experience the physical body you desire. And own your tremendous power to mold your reality from within yourself.

Declaration of Intrinsic Power

Use the following declaration as a template to create your own. Take a moment each day to remind yourself that all the power of change and expansion is within yourself, it's always been within yourself.

I now recognize that the only power in my experience is my own consciousness. Where I once held external conditions and circumstances to be the cause and power in my world, now I know with every fiber of my being that my own consciousness is what matters. My consciousness is what materializes as every moment I experience and this is true for my experience of my physical body and my physical appearance. I need only decide to take my power back, I need only stop assuming that things in the outer world have power over my experiences. And so I do that now.

My consciousness is what determines how my body forms itself for me. My consciousness is what determines how I experience my body and everything related to it. My own consciousness is the source of my physical appearance and form, and so it is here that I do my work.

I am now shifting into a consciousness of health, appreciation, and love for everything about my body. I am now shifting into a consciousness of physical glory. I am now shifting into a consciousness of celebrating the look and feel of my body every moment of my life. And each and every day I grow and grow in my capacity to experience more of my physical health, more of my physical beauty, more of my endless satisfaction with and appreciation for my physical body.

I allow more for the good of my well-being. I allow more for the benefit of those around me. I allow more for the celebration and happiness of my world. As I am fit and well in consciousness, so will I be in my world. As I am radiant in consciousness, so shall I be in my world. And so I am. Here and Now.

And so it is.

New Thoughts

Rehearsing a new set of thoughts is a great way to build a new map for yourself around your body, health, fitness and food. The map you have right now is built on thoughts you have rehearsed in the past and this map can be updated through your active engagement in creating new experiential learning for yourself.

Let yourself really feel the new thoughts as you explore, interact and integrate them. Allow yourself to experience the thoughts and beliefs made available, and create your own positive beliefs using these as your basis.

Pay attention to anything that may come up for you as you engage with these positive thoughts, beliefs and statements about your body, your relationship to your body and your overall approach to health and fitness. If you feel resistance, explore why. Ask yourself "what do I have to believe is true to resist this thought" and see what shows up. The statements included here are only a small representation of the innumerable positive thoughts and beliefs available to you.

Explore, integrate and elevate your mindset. Let go of all that no longer serves you in this area of your experience and step into a completely new mind and perspective on your body and being. Tune into the stream of thinking and feeling that supports your highest and best expression of your body. You can.

General

1. Health, fitness and wellness are my easy reality.
2. Every cell in my body conforms to a blueprint of health, fitness and well-being.
3. Every day and in every way I am becoming fit, healthier and stronger.
4. Being healthy, fit and strong is my default.
5. Every decision I make and every action I take is now aligned to my highest and best.
6. I excel at maximizing my body's full potential.
7. My biological age is decades younger than my chronological age.
8. I give my body the best internal environment in thoughts and emotions to help actualize its potential.
9. This moment and the next I choose health, fitness and total well-being.

10. I am one with the creative force of the cosmos. All the health, fitness and well-being I desire is mine instantaneously and always.
11. My body is a high performing living system with the perfect biochemistry for lasting health and well-being.
12. My body fully supports my need for total health and well-being just as my mind supports my body's need for health and well-being.
13. Health, fitness and wellness are all around me and within me now and always.
14. I now recognize that my body is a dynamic ever-changing living system.
15. It's easy for me to experience my body as a responsive arrangement of light and information.
16. I now only ever look at my body through the lens of love and appreciation.

Ideal Body

17. I am ready and willing to have my ideal body.
18. I am one with my ideal body and my ideal body is now one with me.
19. The reality of my ideal body feels so real and within reach to me right here and now.
20. I am completely okay with living in my ideal body on all levels.

21. I feel good about my new level of fitness, health, size and weight.
22. I love being able to demonstrate to myself that my weight was never about anything other than my energy and vibration.
23. I create my body on all levels. I've always been the one creating my body.
24. I have everything I need to create the body of my dreams right here and right now.
25. My ideal body is a living blueprint I can tap into at any time.
26. It's effortless for me to step into the body of my dreams.
27. I am guided into the right activities for me to live my ideal body now and always.
28. The power to change my body has always been within me. I cease that power now.
29. I choose to be my ideal weight with everything I am. All my past, present, and future selves align together in this choice.
30. I choose to make my dream body a reality right here and right now.
31. My body knows exactly what it needs to do to express my ideal.
32. It's so easy, natural and effortless for me to maintain my ideal weight.
33. I have unconditional massive support from the Universe in achieving and maintaining the body of my dreams for the rest of my life.
34. I feel so much happiness and gratitude for being my ideal weight.

Loving Your Body Now

35. Every day and in every way I love my body more and more.
36. Every day and in every way I feel better and better about my body.
37. I feel marvelous in my body.
38. I enjoy being in my body.
39. I enjoy looking at my body.
40. I shower every part of my body with love and kindness in my thoughts, feelings and through my actions.
41. It's always so easy for me to shape and reshape my body for my highest good.
42. I allow myself to feel really good about my body.
43. I allow myself to feel really good in my body.
44. My ability to love myself just as I am grows and grows.
45. My ability to love my body just as it is grows and grows.
46. I love and accept my body for being so attentive and receptive to my thoughts.
47. I fully and completely trust my body.
48. I treat my body with great love and respect.
49. I've become so good at listening to my body's messages and requests. I am attentive to the feedback my body gives to me every day.
50. I recognize that my body is a sacred temple worthy of love, respect and gratitude.

51. I deeply and completely love, honor and respect my body.
52. I deeply love and appreciate my body for all that it is and for all that it does for me all day every day.
53. I raise the level of love and respect I have for my body.
54. I'm so in love with all that my body does for me and with all that my body makes available to me.
55. My body is a true treasure.
56. I offer my body only the highest and best in all things.
57. My health, my level of fitness, my strength and my sense of aliveness gets better day after day.
58. I breathe in new loving energy and I breathe out and release all the beliefs and memories about my weight that no longer serve me.
59. I let go of any and all limiting beliefs I hold around my body's abilities, my metabolism, and my body's innate intelligence.
60. I enjoy my body so much.
61. My body is an extraordinary creation. I am in awe of all that it does so effortlessly.

Food and You

62. I am honest about my relationship to food.

63. I am awake to all my thoughts, feelings and behaviors around food and with food, around eating and with eating.
64. I now release all tendency to feel negative emotions like guilt and shame around food.
65. I give myself total permission to freely enjoy every morsel of food I mindfully put in my mouth.
66. I now release all unhelpful behavior around food from my mind and body.
67. I now have a healthy and balanced relationship with all food.
68. I create my relationship with food here and now.
69. I am empowered in the relationship I create with food.
70. I choose to have a healthy positive relationship with food.
71. I'm neither addicted nor avoidant of food in all its variety.
72. I choose to feel fulfilled with and without food.
73. I choose to give myself good feelings with and without food.
74. I choose to nourish myself with and without food.
75. Food no longer has any power over me, my decisions and my choices.
76. My body excels at getting everything it needs from the nourishing food I give it.

77. I am attracted to the food that is healing and nourishing for my body.
78. My eating habits support my vision of a healthy fit body.
79. I can easily tell the difference between my body's real need for food and memories of needing food. I can tell the difference easily between real hunger and remembered hunger.
80. I let go of any level of guilt or shame I hold about my old eating habits.
81. I feel healthy, light and awake after every meal. I always only eat the amount of food my body needs to be at its best.
82. I easily and effortlessly recognize that food is not a true source of emotional comfort. I love and care for myself daily and my emotional needs are met in ways that are healthy and loving to my body.
83. I am much more powerful than my eating habits, cravings and food addictions.
84. I feel calm and at ease with or without food.
85. I am mindful and present at every meal. I am present to the vibrancy of the food I consume.
86. Every day and in every way I grow more and more attracted to the foods that support my highest and best.
87. At every meal and with every bite, my body heals, recharges and strengthens.

88. I bless every meal with pure positive energy. I am grateful for the nourishing foods and all that goes into growing and preparing them.
89. I feel and have immense gratitude for all sources of food, from the hands of the farmers that grow my food to the groceries, restaurants and my own kitchen.
90. I feel total and complete freedom around food and eating.

De-constructing the Reality of Weight

Have you come to ask yourself what weight is? Have you come to question what it is that you translate as weight release or weight gain in this time-space environment?

Under the right magnification all that appears as your physical body is pure light. You are only photons and empty space. You are lights waving and wave-patterns lighting. You are weightless at every level of your being. The idea and manifested experience of weight belongs to its own domain of experience, a domain of experience that has its own set of rules of what manifests and how it manifests.

Weight and the experience of weight gain or weight release all belong to the frequency domain of a specific vibrational density. For as long as you view your being through the vibrational lens of physical hard matter of formed, fixed, and unchanging substance, you play by the rules of that vibrational density, that vibrational reality.

Everything in your experience is subject to the rules of the frequency domain in which you participate. Your definitions of who you are and what your physical body is have you tune into a reality field of a specific frequency range. And it is this frequency range that you translate as your day to day experience of physical reality.

As you alter these ideas, as you encode your consciousness-matrix with ideas of a different frequency range, you tune into and become a participator in a reality that is constructed by a different set of rules. There are no limits to how and in what ways you can experience the arrangement of light you translate as your physical body. There are no limits to all that your body can become in this time-space environment.

You are the sole author, definer, and perceiver of all that you make manifest in and as your body and your Universe.

Author's Note

Dear Reader,

Thank you for reading. I hope the ideas and guidance in this workbook helped you to access or reaffirm the wisdom and understanding already within you. My intention with all of my work is that it helps, supports and reinforces your knowing of your power and reminds you of just how cosmically blessed, connected and loved you are. The basis of all that we are is a love that is powerful and a power that is loving.

If you enjoyed this book and would like to do so, please post a short review on Amazon. It is reviews from readers like you that help new readers connect to my work to find the help, support and reinforcement they need in their own empowerment and transformation journey.

Thank you again for joining me in catching up to our collective expansion.

Infinite Blessings to you in all that you are and all that you do.

With great love and gratitude,
Kidest OM

P.S. If you'd like to receive ongoing reminders on your power and potential, you can connect to my social media channels under @KidestOm. I update them fairly regularly with reminders, new insights and more tools, tips and guidance.

About the Author

Kidest OM is the author of a number of books and publications on the power and primacy of consciousness. With a degree in Psychology, and a decade of studying alternative disciplines, Kidest writes and speaks exclusively on consciousness and reality engineering.

She has hosted and created numerous informative radio shows and videos on the subject reaching thousands of viewers and listeners worldwide. Kidest also consults with clients from all over the world through her private coaching and consultation practice.

Currently living in the Pacific North West, Kidest describes life on Vancouver Island as the perfect backdrop to conversations on consciousness.

Made in the USA
Middletown, DE
16 May 2018